THE METAPHORIC MIND
THE METAPHORIC MIND
THE METAPHORIC MIND

A Celebration of Creative Consciousness

. . . . poetry of many kinds . . . gave me great pleasure, and even as a schoolboy I took intense delight in Shakespeare, especially in the historical plays. I have also said that formerly pictures gave me considerable, and music very great, delight. But now for many years I cannot endure to read a line of poetry: I have tried lately to read Shakespeare, and found it so intolerably dull that it nauseated me. I have also lost almost any taste for pictures or music. . . . My mind seems to have become a kind of machine for grinding general laws out of large collections of fact, but why this should have caused the atrophy of that part of the brain alone, on which the higher tastes depend, I cannot conceive . . . . The loss of these tastes is a loss of happiness, and may possibly be injurious to the intellect, and more probably to the moral character, by enfeebling the emotional part of our nature.
— from *Autobiography of Charles Darwin*

THE METAPHORIC MIND
THE METAPHORIC MIND
THE METAPHORIC MIND

A Celebration of Creative Consciousness

Bob Samples

ADDISON-WESLEY PUBLISHING COMPANY

Reading, Massachusetts

Menlo Park, California · London · Amsterdam · Don Mills, Ontario · Sydney

for Stician Marin
who came from us
at solstice time
to a life he will
make.

Ninth Printing, March 1983

Copyright © 1976 by Addison-Wesley Publishing Company, Inc. Philippines copyright 1976 by Addison-Wesley Publishing Company, Inc.

Libary of Congress Cataloging in Publication Data

Samples, Bob.
The metaphoric mind.

Bibliography: p. 211
1. Consciousness.   2. Left and right (Symbolism)
3. Creative ability.   4. Humanistic psychology.
I. Title.
BF311.S34   153.3'5   76-7654

ISBN 0-201-06706-4
IJKLMNOPQR-AL-89876543

All photographs by Bob Samples and Cheryl Charles. Drawings, paintings and collages by Bob Samples. Layout, design and preparation by Bob Samples, Cheryl Charles and Olina Gilbert.

PREFACE

A book about the metaphoric mind is a book about celebration . . . a sensitive, lasting celebration. A companion to humankind through the sweep of time extending from our earliest origins to the moment you read these words. Though about celebration, the story is not without pain and anguish — there has been much of that. It has been experienced by all those who invent . . . who create . . . who see things momentarily (or forever) as no one they know has seen before. By those who find themselves in dissonance with the cultures in which they live. By those who are, in reality, more closely allied to natural systems. Nature is different from culture.

Nature is natural. All of the metaphors — like all of the facets of the human world — can ultimately be traced back to nature. In a myriad of ways humans are now becoming travelers on that journey that leads back into the natural. To ways of knowing not easily explained, that include a celebration of childness and the mystical messages of the emergent species. To the resensitizing of bodies so they can know where the moon is tonight and can feel the messages of the planets and cosmos.

This is not an abandonment of technocracy . . . but rather a taming of technocracy and a reinstatement of natural patterns of celebration and worship. No, not through bizarre rites of sacrifice and lust — those were cultural, not natural — but through the ways that allow us to look through 200 inch telescopes not solely as cultural voyeurs and gatherers of numbers but also as poets, as children of the universe. It is a celebration of the primordial seas we know flow at once through our veins and the tidepools we see before us. It is a way of worship that allows one to stand on a hill looking at the sea with a sense of knowing that all is one. It is worship that lets us know the ironic joke humans alone have played upon themselves by inventing the thing called culture. The irony was not in the invention, for that too was natural . . . instead it was in allowing the offspring to devour the parent.

But the joke is over, the laughter has died down. The metaphoric mind is asking again . . . quietly but insistently . . . for equilibrium. Pain and anguish promise to be balanced by joy and hope. Life and sanity are requiring equilibrium. Equilibrium is the way of nature.

metaph. **1.** Metaphor; metaphorical. **2.** Metaphysics.

met·a·phor (met′ə·fôr, -fər) *n.* A figure of speech in which one object is likened to another by speaking of it as if it were that other, as *He was a lion in battle*: distinguished from *simile* by not employing any word of comparison, such as "like" or "as." **— Syn.** See SIMILE. **— mixed metaphor** A figurative expression in which two or more incongruous metaphors are used, as *He kept a tight rein on his boiling passions*. [< F *métaphore* < L *metaphora* < Gk. < *metapherein* < *meta-* beyond, over + *pherein* to carry] **— met′a·phor′ic** (-fôr′ik, -for′ik) or **·i·cal** *adj.* **— met′a·phor′i·cal·ly** *adv.*

met·a·phys·ic (met′ə·fiz′ik) *n.* Metaphysics. *— adj. Rare* Metaphysical.

met·a·phys·i·cal (met′ə·fiz′i·kəl) *adj.* **1.** Of, pertaining to, or of the nature of metaphysics. **2.** Of or pertaining to ultimate reality or basic knowledge. **3.** Beyond or above the physical or the laws of nature; transcendental.

met·a·phys·ics (met′ə·fiz′iks) *n.pl.* (*construed as sing.*) **1.** The branch of philosophy that investigates principles of reality transcending those of any particular science, traditionally including cosmology and ontology. Compare EPISTEMOLOGY. **2.** All speculative philosophy. **3.** Popularly, abstruse and bewildering discussion. Also *metaphysic*. Abbr. *met., metaph.* [< Med.L *metaphysica* < Med.Gk. < *ta meta ta physika* the (works) after the physics; in ref. to Aristotle's ontological treatises, which came after his *Physics*]

TABLE OF CONTENTS

INTRODUCTION

We live in strange times. Gaining dominance over nature and chance, we are losing precisely those qualities that make life worth living. Fine food and drink are becoming rare, while rationally-organized fast-food chains proliferate. Neither love nor money can buy us the kind of craftsmanship that once was commonplace.

But it's not just amenities that are slipping out of our hands as we become ever more manipulative. The best works of the brightest minds are beginning to backfire. With good intentions, we rip down flimsy, perhaps temporary, slums and replace them with high-rise, institutionalized, permanent slums. To help poor nations, we send them wheat and bulldozers and penicillin, and destroy the social order of a thousand years. To keep each of us alive as long as possible, we create modern medical miracles that bear increasing resemblance to Frankenstein's experiments, while our *good* health drains away, at an exorbitant price.

We live in a technological world that values whatever is hygenic and dust-free and antiseptic. How odd, then, that technology itself has poisoned the air we breathe, the food we eat, the water we drink. Stranger yet is the fact that so many technologists are among those now telling us we must continue our present cancerous, and cancer-producing, rate of growth. To do so, they say, we had best build nuclear reactors that just happen to create, as a by-product, the most toxic substance known to humankind, a poison that remains virulent for tens of thousands of years—this legacy for our children's children, for generations to come.

Those of us who use sweet reason to argue for self-destruction are not evil. We are, rather, the victims of a particularly compelling seduction. Existence has always tempted the human race with extremes, never more so than during the past several centuries. Starting with the Renaissance, the rational/technological/scientific way of doing things has scored one spectacular success after another, and we have followed it with ever-increasing avidity and belief. In the years since Newton, in fact, we have achieved almost every one of the ancient sorcerers' dreams—sailed in the heavens, looked to the other side of the world, floated in space, walked on the moon, transmuted the elements, turned matter into energy. Who can blame us for falling under the spell of such glittering enchantments? It is only that we have fallen too far and have ignored those other aspects of life and mind that make us truly human. Now, if it is not too late, we must wake up to the fact that, in Gregory Bateson's words:

> Mere purposive rationality, unaided by such phenomena as art, religion, dream and the like, is necessarily pathogenic and destructive of life.

Bob Samples' book is by no means anti-rational. It is a powerful, rational argument for re-owning the mind of art, religion, dream and the like: the Metaphoric Mind. At the outset, Samples warns us that his book is "an exaggeration. . .a wild, careening sort of over-statement". With this I cannot agree, for I see *The Metaphoric Mind* as an essay on equilibrium, a plea for a balanced way of thinking and being in a culture that stands on the knife-edge between catastrophe and transformation.

Novelist Wallace Stegner has defined irony as "that curse, that armor, that evasion, that way of staying safe while seeming wise". Bob Samples is not an ironist; he is an enthusiast. Drawing examples and evidence from anthropology, biology, brain physiology, psychology and, best of all, from his own pioneering work in teaching creativity, he writes passionately about the rollicking, intuitive, creative part of ourselves that we have lost and now can find again. *The Metaphoric Mind* is not only a small encyclopedia of transformationalist lore; it is a vivid celebration of human wholeness, a landmark book in the growing literature of positive vision in a dangerous and fascinating age.

GEORGE LEONARD
Author of *The Ultimate Athlete*

We do not have solitary beings. Every creature is, in some sense, connected to and dependent on the rest.

—Lewis Thomas

in the beginning

This book is an exaggeration. It is a wild careening kind of overstatement that opens itself fully to suspicion and criticism. It is like the first steps a child takes compared to the studied, practiced ballet that may come later in life. It is these things and many others because it is an excursion into the most widely traveled but least charted domain that humankind has invented. The ghostlike mystical mind we all possess — the metaphoric mind — contains nature's own expression. It may be stilled with the oceanic silence of the floor of the Mindanao trench. It may scream with the explosiveness of volcanic eruption vented from some fiery place where the earth has failed. It is a world filled with smells and silences and tastes. It contains all the knowing that known things knew. It has within it the way your eyes first felt when you realized you were alive in your mother's womb.

This book is about the metaphoric mind . . . the mirror image of the rational mind. Now that counting has become the passion of so many thousands of nervous humans who seek crashing waves of order and logic and impose them on even the simplest of acts, and audits, accountability, and the ghost of the ultimately balanced checkbook lie over our heads, it is only fitting that there is a world that cannot be measured, a world of mind that resists being counted and one that slips in and out of focus so subtly that we almost forgot it was there.

2

It's not in deep space, or couched inside a buzzing corner of the atom. It's right here with us now. With me, with you. The metaphoric mind has tracked the long journey taken by all the earth's living things as we doubled and trebled and bubbled our way from two tiny slivers of life tumbled into each other's presence by our parents. And it lived in the quiet comforting darkness throughout our journey toward the moments of birth from our mother's womb. It led all of our knowing during those first nine months. There were no words, no orderly structures that could be anything but felt. We breathed in nutrients from the fluids of our mother's ocean . . . and we grew. We lived three and a half billion years during these first nine months and were fully the children of nature . . . particles of the universe.

But once outside, we encounter forceps and stirrups and oceans of tidily wrinkled sterile sheets. There are utensils and pans and clattering chatter. There are masked huge humans. And perhaps there are chemicals and drugs to "make the journey easier." Perhaps the child itself is groggily surging through a chemical stupor fed to it through the soon-to-be-severed umbilicus. In a drawn out, slow-motion charade, like those in the agonized moments of bad dreaming, a hand sweeps in and a silver clamp bites into the child's last link with its natural domain. Then another clamp — and perhaps this is when the screaming starts. The innate sense of losing contact is overwhelming. Then . . .

SNIP!

Our birth is our entry into the world that cultures have built. Now, in the brilliant glare of cultural existence, the fragile tenure of the dominance of the metaphoric mind begins to erode as all the pieces of the rationally-produced culture quietly conspire to push the prevailing natural schemes into the background. The child in utero is not a product of culture . . . it is a parcel of the universe. It is an image of nature.

The child is now of culture. Nature is shoved away and only remains in blurred images when the eyes are closed. It sometimes comes back in sleep . . . but when the eyes open the mind begins to see the new world. This is the world built by the culture. Its richness in structure, in order, in formality begin to encroach upon the ghosted images we as adults have lost.

The child is handed about. If she is awake, the mother looks and sees her companion of two hundred and seventy days. In that fragile moment the first contact with a cultural institution is made. The child swept into being by the impersonal, detached delivery team sees its mother, and as the two cautiously, hesitatingly look at each other, the first of the categories is established: the child becomes culturally a daughter or a son. And then it is gone. Put into another box. A plastic one with a smoothed pad of coldness on its bottom. The child will now be bathed, inspected, sterilized, and stored for safekeeping while mother is repaired and prepared for their first formal meeting.

4

Humans have grown awesomely distant from nature. In the earliest times, the deep affiliation with the natural world created an ecology of metaphor. The mind had not yet created the tools of rational thought. Metaphor prevailed. All things were seen to be related. The natural world and its shifting patterns of change were no more than an extension of the processes that created humans themselves.

Human minds and human bodies were affectionate toward nature. This does not mean that there was a Disneyish kind of "cuddle the cute bears" relationship, but rather that the natural world was the living context of myth, of survival, and of joy. In fact it was out of the earliest searches for rational meanings that the first myths were born. These first myths, the birthplaces of logic, were different from the myths that would come later . . . they were inclusive as opposed to exclusive. The early myths united humans with nature, while the later ones separated humans from nature.

5

The early myths wove a tapestry of affiliation in which the minds, bodies, and souls of humans were no more or less important than the minds, bodies, and souls of tree, sky, or coyote. Humans walked, ran, grew, loved, and died as part of the whole symphony of life. All things were alive. Thousands of years would pass before rational thought would dominate and force humans into deciding that some things were alive and some were dead. Once this distinction was made, it would be easy to decide that some living things were more important than others, and they would begin to *use* these living things as though they had dominion over them. Thus they would interrupt the natural rhythms and substitute a designed, artificial cadence.

With this most fateful of decisions, the mythologies shifted. The stories that wedded the generations together would become ritualistic examples of humans tricking, manipulating, and finally conquering nature. At the same time, tools were created and humans began the long evolutionary process that converted the digging stick into the bulldozer.

Somewhere . . . lost in the past . . . at some moment between when humans cut the umbilicus that had linked them with nature and when they invented the artificial ecology — culture — humans made another fateful decision. This new decision is considered by many to have been the greatest of moments in human history. It gave humans the capacity to rule over nature: they would gain the power to "go into the wilderness, be fruitful and multiply." This decision would allow the hunting and gathering clans to settle down, to relax, and to create a kind of stability. The decision? *Humans planted the first seeds.*

SNIP!

Agriculture, often considered a turning point in human history, marked the beginnings of the shift away from the metaphoric mind. It was the death of the hunting and gathering society. Turning to agriculture, humans stopped being a part of nature and started to become the masters of nature. A task that swept down centuries of development to the statement, "One small step for man, one giant step for mankind." The seed grew.

With harvests came surplus. With surplus came storage. Places had to be created to store the surpluses and so warehouses were built. The keepers of the warehouses were the trusted elders of the tribe. Their role evolved quickly into priesthood and they became counselors of ethics and justice. Almost at once the warehouse became the seat of religion — the church — and the court.

SNIP!

Religion and law require rules — too many rules to depend upon remembering them via the spoken story-telling route. Some way of preserving the ancient stories had to be found. The Sumerians found a way. Their location was rich in tillable land in the Valley of the Tigris-Euphrates, and they used it well. The surpluses gave them the most overwhelming abundance known to any people living at their time. Because of these surpluses the Sumerian presence exploded into a network of villages, towns, and cities that far down the corridor of time would be known as Civilization. But there was still one vital ingredient missing . . . so they invented it. It was writing.

SNIP! SNIP! SNIP!

The earliest cuneiform writings of the Sumerians were warehouse inventories. They were accounts of the wealth that abundance had accumulated. Later, according to some scholars, in times of crisis or abundance the warehouse keepers began to record the stories by using this new-found technology. The discovery was amazing: one could substitute symbols for reality! The joy of this awareness resulted in an avalanche of cuneiform tablets that told the stories of creation, of crises, of history. Rules and ethical strategies were written down. Laws and commandments were born that bear such striking similarity to contemporary Western religions that most current practitioners are forced to acknowledge these distant early origins.

Now bathed and anointed, her first ritual, and labeled with a plastic bracelet, her first jewelry, baby daughter is brought back, diapered in her first clothing, to a strange blend of nature and culture called . . . *mother*. Numbers have been recorded. Time of birth, weight, length. Names of parents, a code number to match bracelet with crib. Billing records are all in some folder along with doctors' names, members of the delivery team, credit ratings, and appointment records. Automatic counters metered any necessary flow of oxygen through steel bottles inventoried, labeled, and recorded not only at the hospital but at the supplier's, several shippers', and in manufacturing plants a thousand miles away. The baby girl is already the peak of an Everest of records and numbers and notations that started with the first seeds. The ones in Sumer and the ones in her mother's womb.

By this time a whole gaggle of people who are part of the child's family are usually involved. The father has probably seen the child by now, perhaps only through glass in the nursery. But now, if he dons a surgical mask and a gown, he can go into the room where the mother's body is rapidly processing the drugs she has received to bring her body back to a "natural" state. The last numbness will leave the area of her vagina where the steel of the scissors snipped the muscle so that the child's entry into culture would be more "efficient." At first the mother may not recognize the father in his surgical mask, but she deeply "knows" the child. Most often as mother and child look at each other, their whole bodies still resonating with the ecstasy of having known the intimacy of oneness, there is the most beautiful conscious awareness they may ever have the opportunity to share . . . Then the moment is broken.

"Who do you think she looks like?"

No one can say where the question will come from. It may be from one of the parents or from the vicarious technological mother, the nurse who did the first ritual bathing, the jeweling, and the clothing. But none the less it will come. The child is out. It is no longer natural. It is in the culture. It is *she*. *She* is part of a family. *She* is *daughter*. *She* is the last statistic on a long delta of genealogical charts that start in Sumer.

She is now in a world that benignly prefers her being a part of *it* rather than it being a part of *her*. She singly has been responsible for part of the lives of those thousands of impersonal people who accumulated all the records, made all the goods, deliveries, and mistakes, and turned all the machines on and off. But now that she is here, the culture demands she be part of it. All its forces are gathered to influence her, coerce her, and mold her into its latticework. All those whose lives touched her statistics do not know she is here . . . save those last few. But even now they are preparing for the next statistic. The second hand on the delivery room clock is moving steadily toward the next integer.

The child is now with her parents. She and they will share the natural for a time. There will be long moments of touching, of loving, and of unspoken awareness of their natural bonds. But even as they cuddle her and pledge to keep this moment's intimacy forever, the schedules of culture appear. Rationality and logic slip in and the child's naturalness and purity of metaphoric existence are interrupted. The woman in white returns and says, "She has to go back now," and her schedules begin. The natural rhythms of her mother's heartbeat, eating, lovemaking, and walking are gone forever. Now come the new ones, all ticking to some clock and calendar of contrivance. *Their* schedule, *their* rules, *their* convenience. As she is carried out her metaphoric mind hears another rational question by the nurse . . . "What did you decide to name her?"

SNIP!

14

memory

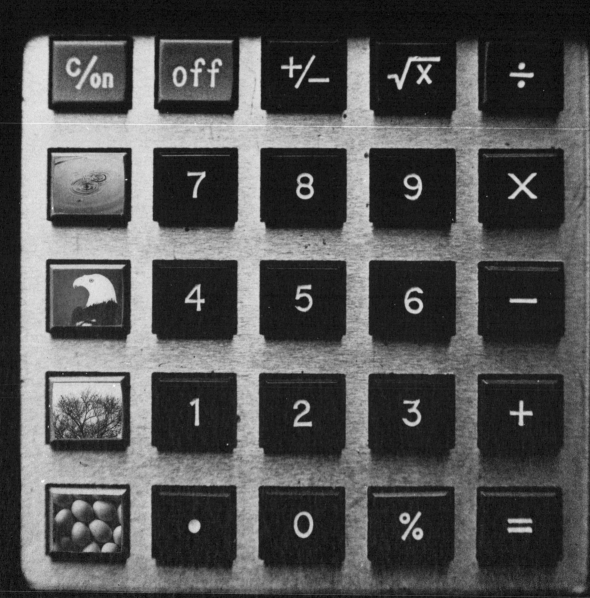

We must first extend the boundaries of inquiry of modern science,
extend our concept of what is possible for man.

—Robert Ornstein

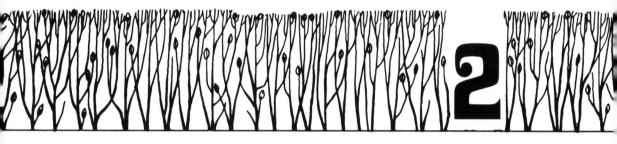

the rational side of metaphor

Whether the metaphoric mind exists is no longer a serious question.
The intuitive awareness of its presence appears far back in history with
the emergence of the first prejudices about right- and left-handedness.
The left hand was always the possessor of less virtue than the right. The
functions of each hand were linked to ways of knowing. Even in those
Sumerian stories referred to earlier, right-handedness carried with it the
approval of the culture. It was predictable, hard-working, aggressive,
dependable — in a word, conforming. Conformity is necessary for
cultures. The rules, the established ways of doing things, must be
preserved or they change . . . and the culture evolves. Thus conformity
upholds cultural stability while deviance or alteration does, in fact,
destroy the culture. Right-handedness was the preserving influence and
left-handedness the deviator.

16

More than a hundred years ago, handedness became linked to "brainedness" by objective scientific criteria. The nervous system, acting like an upside-down tree, was seen to spread its branches fully throughout the body with its base gathered together in the wrinkled nut-like form of the brain. There the network twisted about on itself in such a way that the left side of the body, along with the "sinister" hand, was connected to and influenced by the right side of the brain. Conversely, the right hand and body side was linked to the left side of the brain.

Artists, poets, and playwrights are among those who have been credited with influencing cultural change. As history progressed they usually became identified with "left"-handed knowing. Not surprisingly, the opposite was true for lawmakers, priests, and technologists. Their stabilizing influence wedded them to the right and righteous mode. They were logical, predictable, and thus rational. It was with metaphor — with the arts — that ambiguity and deviance came. And with rationality came stability and logic.

17

Recently a great many scientific researchers have verified and elaborated upon these differences in the qualities of the mind's work. Studies representing more than a century of research have verified that these two different qualities of mind are housed in opposite cerebral hemispheres. The brain's left cerebral hemisphere is the model of "right-handedness." It houses the organizing, logical, "conforming" qualities. It strings things together sequentially in language and in linear time sequences. And it worries a lot about the rules of reading, writing, and arithmetic. It sees things discretely and its processes tend to converge toward the single most logical outcome in a series of thoughts. And, as was said before in the context of a cultural setting, most often logic and rationality are determined by that which is most stable and most conforming.

The right cerebral hemisphere in most people is the residence of the metaphoric mind. This is the "left-handed" domain. When an idea comes into the metaphoric mind, a sudden rush of relationships flashes into being and the original thought expands rapidly outward into a network of new holistic perceptions. The role of metaphoric thinking is to invent, to create, and to challenge conformity by extending what is known into new meadows of knowing. The metaphoric mind treats all input as fragments of reality, and as soon as a fragment appears the mind begins the search for the whole. Like an archaeologist who discovers a shard, a tiny fragment of an ancient pot, the metaphoric mind at once begins to visualize the whole creation.

What I am calling the metaphoric mind has had dozens of comparisons with its partner, the rational mind. As I have indicated, some awarenesses of the metaphoric mind go back thousands of years. A good compilation of the characteristics of these two modes of knowing was assembled by Robert Ornstein in his marvelous book, *The Psychology of Consciousness*. His comparisons are shown in the table.

Who Proposed It?		
Many sources	Day	Night
Blackburn	Intellectual	Sensuous
Oppenheimer	Time, History	Eternity, Timelessness
Deikman	Active	Receptive
Polanyi	Explicit	Tacit
Levy, Sperry	Analytic	Gestalt
Domhoff	Right (side of body)	Left (side of body)
Many sources	Left hemisphere	Right hemisphere
Bogen	Propositional	Appositional
Lee	Lineal	Nonlineal
Luria	Sequential	Simultaneous
Semmes	Focal	Diffuse
I Ching	The Creative: heaven masculine, Yang	The Receptive: earth feminine, Yin
I Ching	Light	Dark
I Ching	Time	Space
Many sources	Verbal	Spatial
Many sources	Intellectual	Intuitive
Vedanta	Buddhi	Manas
Jung	Causal	Acausal
Bacon	Argument	Experience

19

Richard Jones added to this list of pairs from the perspective of a psychotherapist, in a talk he recently gave in Denver*:

Freud	Secondary Process	Primary Process
Piaget	Primary Symbolism	Secondary Symbolism
Piaget	Accommodation	Assimilation
Schactel	Conventionalized Experience	Trans-schematic Experience
Maslow	A Cognition	B Cognition
Taylor	Convergent Thinking	Divergent Thinking
Langer	Discursive Symbolism	Presentational Symbolization
Polanyi	Focal Awareness	Subsidiary Awareness
Neisser	Sequential Processing	Multiple Processing
Kubie	Conscious Processing	Preconscious Processing
Wertheimer	Productive Thinking	Blind Thinking
Bleuler	Realistic Thinking	Autistic Thinking
Many sources	Public Knowledge	Private Knowledge
Many sources	Literal Meaning	Metaphorical Meaning

These compilations cannot help but emphasize the variety of perspectives from which this issue has been viewed over the years. There has never been an absence of historical insight to encourage the kind of research that is now being pursued.

*Jones, Richard M. *Looking Back and Forth on Consciousness*. Prepared as the keynote address for the Invitational Conference of the Social Science Education Consortium, Inc., June 13, 1975.

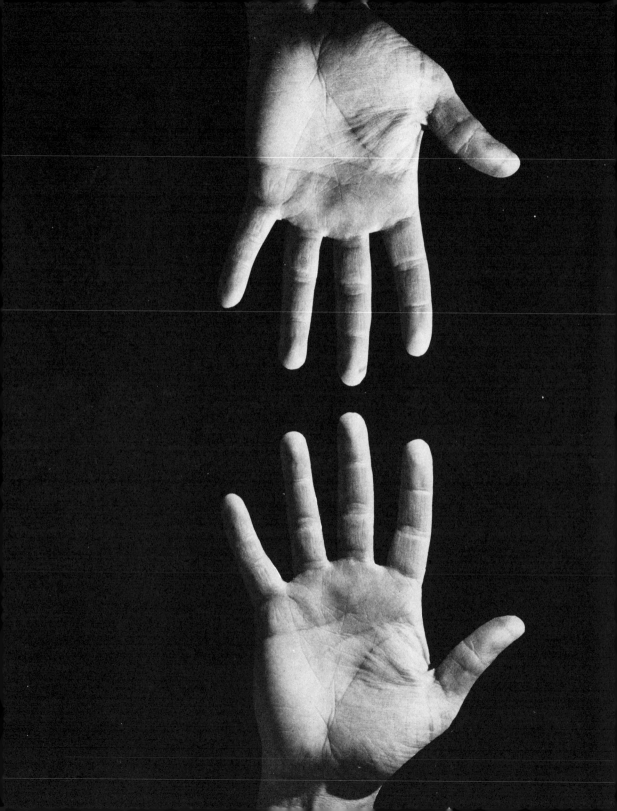

The research that adds credence to the differences in the functions represented above has until recently come primarily from study of humans whose brains had been somehow damaged. Victims of automobile accidents, warfare, and injuries of a variety of sorts had paraded before the watchful eyes of physicians for years. The great store of data that accumulated began to indicate clearly that very specific kinds of handicaps would result if certain parts of the brain were damaged.

Left hemisphere damage interferes with language, writing, analytic thinking, and ordering of objects or symbols in sequence. For years physicians and physiologists have called this hemisphere the "major" one, as any damage to it seemed to interfere mightily with those qualities of mind work our culture cherishes. Thus those people whose early research charted the continents of the brain were as culturally biased as those who early explored the geography of the earth.

If the "minor" or right hemisphere was the locus of damage, then one often lost the ability to draw, create music, and visualize spatial relationships, and frequently also suffered an impairment in depth perception. Some who suffered damage to the right hemisphere couldn't do visual or tactile maze puzzles. More recent research has been performed on humans via corrective surgery for a variety of disorders. The surgery involves the cutting of the corpus callosum, a thick bundle of connecting nerve conduits that allows information to pass easily between the hemispheres. This connection is the primary channel through which the rational and metaphoric minds can communicate. A second link exists through the eyes. Both eyes are connected to both cerebral hemispheres via a split in the optic nerve.

Surgery that separates the hemispheres by severing the corpus callosum and the optic nerve linkages dramatically shows the differences between the minds. This surgery was originally performed on epilepsy victims in an effort to lower the uncontrollable feedback between the hemispheres during a seizure. The results were dramatic and successful, with very few noticeable side effects. Seldom did the patients show changes in personality. Most of their everyday living and working functions appeared unimpaired. And yet the seizures diminished remarkably.

The differences in function these studies and others have demonstrated are being researched vigorously. Each day new data are being gathered not only about the details of specialization within each of the two minds but also concerning how this specialization takes place over time. David Galin at the Langley-Porter Neuropsychiatric Institute of the University of California Medical Center is examining the specialization of the two hemispheres over time. His careful plan involves assessing which hemisphere is working when different mental tasks are performed. To do this he is using a series of highly sophisticated biofeedback devices which monitor the electrical energy produced by minds in action. Some of these devices measure energy produced in the brain, and others detect the brain's influence on the skin, eyes, and other areas of the body. It has been known for a long time that the minds of infants are not differentiated. Their minds, not yet affected by the culture in which they live, are almost totally metaphoric. Furthermore, the corpus callosum is not yet constricted, and the two hemispheres are nearly mutually blended together in a single brain. As growth takes place and the brain increases in size, the relative size of the connecting linkages seems to decrease. This may just be the effect of both hemispheres growing on both sides of a conduit that remains the same size as it was in infancy. However, not only does the size of the connecting linkages seem to change, but so too does their quality. They appear to get more compressed, firmer, and the smooth "open window" connection becomes a fibrous filter between the minds. This seems to happen at some time between three and four years of age.

What Galin and his colleagues hope to determine is related to just *when* the specialization takes place. They hope to gather data on people of all ages from infancy to the mid-teens. In addition, plans have been discussed to carry out a series of observations of individual humans from infancy to adolescence. Such longitudinal studies will provide a rational data base that does not now exist.

We can speculate with rather high certainty about the expected results. *The specialization of the hemispheres of the brain into what I refer to as the two minds is the result of acculturation.* The child entering the world with an unspecialized metaphoric mind is a child of nature. Time is cyclic; space is limitless; all things are holistic and unified. But shortly after birth culturation begins. Language is the dominant cultural influence, and it introduces the child to its first cultural discovery: the undifferentiated, holistic world it perceives cannot be communicated holistically. It must first be chopped up and labeled.

Words are attached to objects, to conditions, to experience. The child sees the world that was once unseparated transformed into a world that becomes many separate and discrete entities. There is mommy, there is daddy, there is hot, there is cold. Food, potty, cry, smile, sleep, and play all become shards of a world that the mind once blended together in a private metaphoric universe. The metaphoric mind in infants is a private mind. The rational mind begins to form when the private mind goes public. Language is the primary medium of the public mind. Language is the first linearity in a world controlled by logic, order, sequence, and interdependent structure.

24

As the child grows, language use increases steadily. Once the act of carving up the universe into labeled parcels is carried out, the child is confronted with the notion that these word-pieces of the world can be strung together in necklaces of meaning. The child's second great cultural discovery is that not only is the world fragmented, but the fragments can be manipulated. Sentences are born.

Shortly after the first sentences are uttered and practiced and polished . . . and the child learns that she can make things happen with words strung together, then the third great cultural discovery is made. There is a game plan to the stringing of word-necklaces. *They are supposed to be strung together in certain ways. Grammar.* At about the same time that this third great cultural discovery is made, the corpus callosum is about to complete its genetic mandate to separate the minds.

The corpus callosum goes through its developmental stages regardless of cultural influence. Physiologically, the developing brain responds to messages encoded in the DNA, and as growth proceeds this fibrous barrier becomes more distinct. One question that will plague many psychological researchers for years to come is the issue of what role the corpus callosum plays. Does it *cause* the brain to be separated into the different functions, or is it a relatively innocent bystander?

My feeling is that it is primarily neutral in the process. In cultures that do not have a dominant compulsion toward linear, rational languages, there appears to be less differentiation of cerebral functions. To me the issue is not that a corpus callosum exists, but that we have a cultural bias which nurtures the separation of the rational and metaphoric minds. Further, the culture in which we live is prejudiced against one of them. The accepted medium of communication, language, is the most dominant mechanism for implementing this prejudice. As stated earlier, rationality requires order, logic, and sequence — qualities that our culture labels grown-up, mature, and adult.

The metaphoric mind is a maverick. It is as wild and unruly as a child. It follows us doggedly and plagues us with its presence as we wander the contrived corridors of rationality. It is a metaphoric link with the unknown called religion that causes us to build cathedrals — and the very cathedrals are built with rational, logical plans. When some personal crisis or the bewildering chaos of everyday life closes in on us, we often rush to worship the rationally-planned cathedral and ignore the religion. Albert Einstein called the intuitive or metaphoric mind a sacred gift. He added that the rational mind was a faithful servant. It is paradoxical that in the context of modern life we have begun to worship the servant and defile the divine.

In a world in which men write thousands of books and one million scientific papers a year, the mythic *bricoleur* is the man who plays with all that information and hears a music inside the noise.
—William Irwin Thompson

metaphors of cycle and line

Language and its use provide the most powerful structure a culture can devise to guide and constrain the function of mind. From the time the child said her first words and thus began the process of fragmenting her perception, she started playing a game the rules of which were written by a cultural prejudice in favor of abstraction. It is a prejudice that will follow her from crib to kindergarten to Ph.D. and beyond. As I said earlier, the first cultural discovery is the realization that all experience, all feeling, all objects, and all qualities of living can be fragmented and isolated by word labels. The very process of creating such codified meanings is of itself an abstraction. In the "game" of rational abstraction, this act of labeling is equivalent to identifying the players in sports contests. It is the "you can't know the culture without a score card" syndrome.

The second great cultural discovery cited in the last chapter is that these "players" can be organized into teams to achieve certain goals, including the manipulation of future events. There are even rules governing the way the teams can play, and language goes beyond this "team play" and beyond simple fragmentation. Somehow there seems to be a strangely inherent compassion within language which resists the notion that the world be left as a chaotic pile of labels. Language carries within it the tacit hope that the labels will be recemented back into more appropriate holistic form.

Thus the pieces become sentences, and their relationships with each other become wedded to some mysterious set of rules called grammar. Grammar is logical. It is the child's first real introduction to the concept of logic. And logic is the myth of the Western technocratic world. Logic is the myth, and rationality is the religion.

By learning language — its words, its structure, and its grammar — the child begins to experience the prevailing myth of Western culture. Like all myths, logic is mystical and ethereal at first. It does not seem threatening at all. It is really fun to look full in the face of the natural world and draw little word boundaries around all its pieces. There's a joy that children experience in the mastery of those first word-reality linkages. They squeal and smile, darting about labeling everything in sight with words. This is dog. That is cat. Here is floor. There is roof. People get labeled too . . . sister, brother, mommy, daddy, aunt, and uncle. The world is a pile of nouns.

Soon words emerge for things that cannot be seen . . . words like hot and cold, near and far, wait and come. The child begins to know such things are special. They have rules that go beyond just labeling. They are related to *how* things are, not just *what* they are. This is where the structure comes in. Some kinds of words tell you *about* something. Others tell you to *do* something. The child begins to try to sort all of this out. And this act of sorting is the birth of the major involvement that the one- or two-year-old child will have for the next eighteen years of life in this culture.

Jerome Bruner, long interested in the psychology of learning, calls language acquisition the most profound learning act the child will *ever* demonstrate. And he adds a somewhat unnerving clarifier, stating that *no one knows how it takes place.* Yet most of the cultural institutions — family, school, and church — all do what they can to assist the child in gaining new words, new meanings, in refining language use, and finally . . . in becoming more logical. Generally the more logical children become with language use, the more "success" they can expect in this culture. They are not held back in school. They get better grades, thus more approval, and have a better chance to stay in the game longer. In other words, they will probably continue their schooling through college and have entry into the final rites of incubation, graduate school.

But occasionally cultures experience anxiety. Most often their collective anxieties emerge when some kind of inexplicable change is taking place. In the face of things not easily explained, cultures do become, quite metaphorically, *nervous.* It's no coincidence that when the nervousness of a culture is felt in educational circles, arguments reflexively emerge about reading, writing, and arithmetic. "Back to the basics" is the somewhat nostalgic response of people who begin to see the minds of children wander into metaphor. Wandering into metaphor makes people nervous.

Bruner and his colleague Irven DeVore, both then of Harvard, were struck by the fact that primates all seem to have long periods of incubation after infants are born. There are extended periods of training and "schooling" that are not matched by other animals such as cats and dogs. The longest of these extended incubation patterns is found, of course, in humans. Although physical and sexual maturity is reached between ten and thirteen years for most humans, the formal or approved of entrance into culture is usually postponed for a decade beyond that.

The culture knows . . .

31

Returning for a moment to a child acquiring language in this culture, recall that I referred to this as a "sorting out" process. The act of sorting out is vital to understanding the separation of the rational and metaphoric minds. Although it is not necessary to know the names of apples and oranges to know they are edible, the names are necessary to separate them from each other and from grapes and tangerines. In fact the act of labeling any parcel of nature is to separate it from others. This act of semantic surgery quickly develops into a strategy of mind function that has at its core an act in opposition to holism and synthesis. Thus from a surprisingly simple beginning spring the roots of those qualities of mind function that grow and blossom into the two minds that researchers logically verify today.

Another avenue toward this same conclusion has been explored by Alexander Marshack in his *Roots of Civilization*, soon to become a classic. In this book, Marshack speculates that in early hunting and gathering societies, spoken language was formalized to the point that organizing and symbolizing processes developed. Though writing in abstract or pictorial form had not yet come on the scene, its precursors had. Art, stories, and rites had become part of the cultures. As these early shadows in the history of humankind flickered on the walls of future cultures, logic began to assume its crystalline form.

Marshack was a journalist assigned to the task of writing a history of the moon shots. In the course of his research he dove deeply into the history of humankind in an effort to find the first recorded beginnings of human interest in the sky. Not satisfied with the traditional records that credited the emergent civilizations of Egypt, Sumeria, India, and Asia, Marshack looked for more distant roots.

His pursuit eventually led him to a small fragment of bone found in a district called Ishango in east Africa. The scratches on the bone at first intrigued Marshack and then consumed him. He lost his sense of commitment to the writing and shifted it with great fervor to the study. The Ishango bone was "neanderthal" or early paleolithic in terms of age. No one had ever suggested a linear notation system for humans of that dawning era. What I mean by linear, of course, refers to logical notation — that kind of ordering of observations and events into systems of communication that "make sense" to all who use them. It's the kind of logic that most historians assigned *only* to those humans who left a written legacy of their experience.

Not only had no one before suggested that early humans had such a linear notation system, but there was a tacit kind of chauvinism aimed at early paleolithic humans that by innuendo styled them "cave men" and thus dismissed them from the serious work of many scholars.

Not so with Marshack. First of all he was not a scholar in the traditional sense of the word. He was a novice. His naïveté was his forte. He didn't know that he wasn't supposed to be interested in what kind of logic or linear notation the early paleolithic people had. Because he had not been schooled otherwise, he assumed the Ishango notches of different width, length, and spacing *meant* something. So he studied them. He said:

I looked at the photos and drawings of the bone for perhaps an hour, thinking. I got up for coffee, still thinking, and came back. How does one "decode" or translate or interpret scratch marks 8,500 years old, created by a culture that was dead and by a man who spoke a language that was lost? Scratch marks that had been made 2,000 to 3,000 years before the first hieroglyphic writing? And, besides, what proof could there be of any interpretation? As Dr. Leroi-Gourhan had suggested, we seemed to be forever stuck in the realm of guesswork and imagination.

What went on inside me for that hour was odd. I was churning with the broad, encompassing insights of an unfinished book, and I was disagreeing with an interpretation that seemingly went against what I had written. It was a dull, blackened bit of scratched bone, about three and three-quarter inches long (9.6 cm), and would one day end up in a museum under glass, with a caption, probably, about the enigmatic, undecipherable activities of prehistoric man.

I decided to try a hunch, based on ideas suggested by the book I was writing. In fifteen minutes I had "cracked the code" of the Ishango bone. Or at least, I felt I had come close to it. I was dizzied.*

---

*Marshack, Alexander. *The Roots of Civilization*. McGraw Hill, New York, 1972, pp. 15,16.

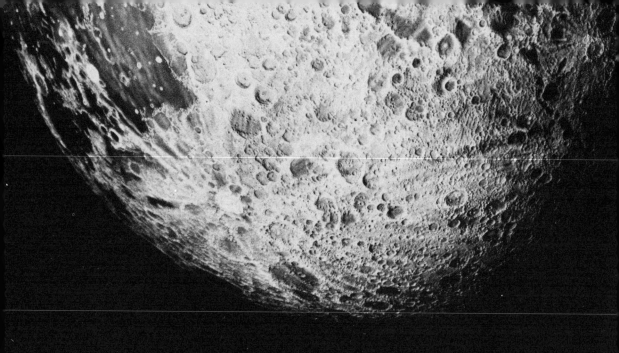

Marshack trusted his metaphoric mind. So he went with it. One can only fantasize that the gift it provided was stored in ways of processing that were systematically rejected by the logic of scholarship for decades. In fact a world-renowned scholar, upon receiving a phone call from Marshack, listened patiently to the journalist's excited interest in early paleolithic notation systems. When Marshack was finished the scholar dryly stated, "There are no early paleolithic notation systems." The pause that followed was quickly filled up with Marshack's enthusiasm and he won the interest of the scholar who invited him to France to provide a further demonstration of his hypothesis. Within days Marshack had clearly shown that he had made a major discovery. Neanderthal Man had made lunar charts. The Ishango bone was the first linear statement about a natural cycle in the known history of humankind.

What Marshack had really done was to pinpoint the first known record of logical record-keeping. He may have found the birthplace of Western thought on this diminutive bone in Africa. The birth of logical thought was needed before logic and linearity could form the structure of language. It is useless to argue which came first, logical notation of natural systems or the logic of language, but they undoubtedly came far earlier than most scholars had thought. The traditional view of spoken language as the transmitter of cultural heritage was to disappear.

Storied thought was told in storied time. It was amorphous and cyclical in pattern. It was enriched by personal experience and personal talent. It was rich in metaphor, and the images were undoubtedly the images of nature. Marshack (pp. 117,118) elaborates on the transition toward more linear thought as follows:

Once voice and brain had evolved to the point where the hominid could utter syllabic words, these words would not, in the early stage, have been used as *defined* symbols, abstracted in meaning, as we define words today in a dictionary or in a course in a foreign language where one word refers to, or is compared with, another word. Nor would words have been used merely to "name" things. On the contrary, it would seem that the words would, in large measure, have been used *as part* of a communication of meaning that could be understood only within a process or relation, or if they referred to a process or relation. Only then could words be symbolic and be understood in reference to the non-verbal process or relation. A cry or a specialized word of warning at the presence of a carnivore is perhaps the simplest example. But the non-verbal content of such a process or relation would *always* have had a meaning more important and inclusive than could ever be contained in the word or words . . .

The word, then, like the stone tool and fire, was an adjunct and a product of the increasingly complex, widening, time-factored, time-factoring capacity and potential of the hominine brain and its culture.

As I have indicated, though a word and the knowledge it referred to would often have been specific to a valley and a hunting group, the ability and the potential were innate and were becoming *increasingly generalized* . . .

It would also follow that fear, threat, pain, anger, frustration, hunger, illness, dependence, desire, puberty, menstruation, old age — that is, expressable or recognizable emotional or physical states — would, at different stages, also find component words or gestures. Such communication concerning hominoid states would also entail a common awareness that was essentially time-factored and non-verbal, referring to processes and relations with a large measure of emotional, kinesthetic, or mimetic understanding . . .

The Ishango bone metaphorically brought storied time to an end. It took the phases of the moon once experienced only visually or from memory and substituted an abstract codification for these phases in the form of scratches of differing widths and length. But even more — the scratches were made in sequential, linear order.

Marshack's contribution could rest upon this awareness alone, but he goes on to provide an even more exciting medium for understanding these phenomena. Time. Time is perceived in two ways . . . as a cycle or as a line. Cyclic time is the time image that best applies to nature. Seasons, days, seeds, and birth-death cycles are all part of the rhythmic pulse of nature. Linear time is an abstraction. It is the invention of humans who arbitrarily divide up cycles into units. Unfortunately once the division is made, the units are often perceived as being more significant than the cycles. They are, after all, more logical . . . that is, they are more addable, subtractable, and certainly more abstract. Cycles, on the other hand, vary. None of the cycles of nature occur consistently in terms of linear time. Days, tides, seasons, and gestation periods are all different in terms of linear time. As a result they pose problems to those who measure them in linear time — the rational thinkers. They pose no problems to those who accept cyclic time, for these humans are closer to nature and to the metaphoric mind.

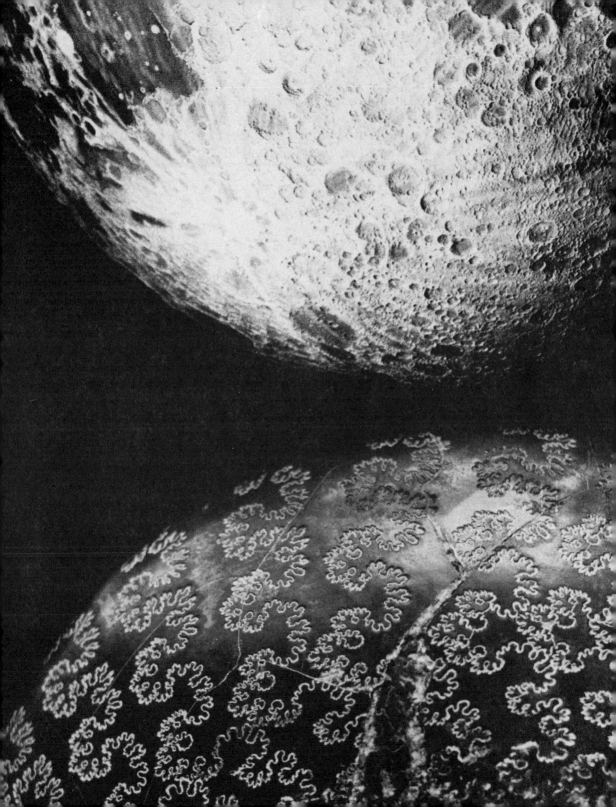

At a recent meeting sponsored by the National Science Foundation, I heard a noted scientist talk about a test for young people that was supposed to diagnose their awareness of concepts in science. It was a true/false test, and one of the questions paired these two statements:

Which is true?
Seeds eat birds.
Birds eat seeds.

The scientist went on to explain that if the children answered that "seeds eat birds," he could proceed to correct their mistake. I interrupted with the claim that seeds in fact *do* eat birds if one waits long enough. One must, however, know enough about natural systems to understand this. The process of living life from birth to death is one of cycling through natural systems. As birds die, they naturally decay into the soil, adding their substance as potential nutrients for living matter to follow. That seeds might naturally find their way into this soil and subsequently sprout into healthy plants having "eaten" the birds and other nutrients in the soil, is a real possibility. Some children know this . . . some know it through metaphoric or cyclic awareness.

At the meeting mentioned above, however, the argument that followed my claim was a classic example of the difference between linear interpretation and cyclic interpretation. That scientist was a physicist — a master of symbolic, abstract logic. Prior to focusing in psychology, I had studied geology and astrophysics. I was prejudiced toward cycles and cyclical thinking. Neither of us could feel fulfilled in the discussion. He could not acknowledge the naturalness of cyclical thought, and I could not convince him that linearity is but a fragment of a cycle.

39

In our cultural heritage the explosion of logic and the documented historical birthplace of rationality was with the Greek civilizations. So many of the shibboleths carved upon the entrances of libraries and universities are traceable to those ancients who perfected linearity on the slopes of Euclid's world. They wrote the Western cookbook of logic. Science was born when humans began to understand that a cycle was far less anxiety-producing if one snipped a piece out of it and studied the piece in the absence of the rest. This was the way of linearity. Just as the child learns word-labels and word-necklaces, meanings, and sentences by separation, so too did early science apply reductive strategies to the universe of nature. To lessen the chaos of cycles, linearity had to emerge as a process. Finer and finer increments of perception had to be created. Instruments that refined this fineness were needed; microscopes, telescopes, and units of measurement were needed.

This process is best summed up by philosopher David Hawkins:

> According to general belief, science — or, at any rate, good science — is necessarily quantitative. A dubious corollary states that by being quantitative one will, inevitably, develop good science. When a science, or some part of a science, has failed to develop rapidly and surely, it is often said that what is needed is the introduction of quantitative methods. The argument is familiar in the literature of biology, geology, economics, sociology, etc. It has even been heard, from time to time, in political science, history, and ethics. So strong is the belief in the efficacy of measurement as the gateway to science that it becomes a kind of badge in office. In American universities at the present time one finds a sort of academic pecking order based upon the prevailing accuracies and austerities of measurement. In the entrance hall of one university's physics building are displayed the "really basic" standards of measurement: the meter stick, the kilogram, and the pendulum. Physics pecks first.[*]

Measurement, exactness, linearity . . . none are bad, none are good, they simply *are*. Part of what they are is related to our mind strategies as approved of by our culture. Another is in their being inevitably a part of environments that are manifestly removed from nature. A day loses its connotation of a single earth-spin and instead it becomes twenty-four hours. Eight of these are spent working, eight are spent sleeping, and eight are usually considered wasted as they usually interfere with the other two. Just as the journey from conception to birth is a parade of all things that lived before us, so too is the acquisition of language a drama of the whole cultural evolution of Western civilization.

[*]Hawkins, David. *The Language of Nature*. W. H. Freeman Co., San Francisco, 1964, p. 87.

Marshack alludes to the dominance of cyclical awareness, the metaphoric mind, up to a point near 10,000 years ago, when the stories, the myths, and the telling of them created the cultural germ plasm of linearity. That transformation resulted in a growing preference for linearity in the cultural setting. This joyous explosion of linear dominance can only be considered the cultural precedent for the individual child bursting into the delight of acquiring a language and its attendant linearities. The acquisition of rational dominance is fun. At least it is fun for a while.

The eventual price of giving up the metaphoric mind may well be too high, for it results in the severing of the umbilicus of humankind from nature. That separation contains the most awesome of responsibilities. It means the creation of a world in which humans live in nearly total linear abstraction. A world of artifice and synthetic realities, in which the most pessimistic sees a dead planet infected by glass and steel blisters shot through by pneumatic tubes leading to artificially lighted cysts in its interior. Linearity will have won and cyclic thinking will have died. And humankind . . .?

The contrasting worlds of cycle and line are real. So too is the separation of function in the cerebral hemispheres. In effect the left cerebral hemisphere is specialized to process linear time. The right hemisphere is specialized to house an awareness of the cyclical. In Ornstein's metaphors, this separation of task is a reflection of cultural divergence as well. The logic and linearity of the Western mind is nourished by the sequential fragmentation of time and space in the Ishango-born left hemisphere. The holism and vivid acceptance of cyclical thought so typical of the Eastern mind resides in the right hemisphere.

Philosophy and psychology are often difficult to separate. When one studies psychology in a Western culture, the philosophy of that culture affects one's perceptions as surely as the natural conditions of climate and geology combine to control the plants that grow in a particular place. My culture, my language, and the logical relationship between the two affect the ways I think. My thoughts are likewise affected as I attempt to communicate them to you through the words and images on these pages.

In our culture, psychology is in a state of rapid transition. It is moving from simplistic linearities toward more holistic kinds of theories. The trends are clear. The human mind is beginning to resist describing itself only by those qualities that can be objectively measured. However, the traditions of linearity are powerful in psychology. In the next chapter, I trace my view of the nature of the dominant linear quality of psychological perceptions . . . those psychological perceptions that are most influential in the descriptions of the rational mind.

This is what intelligence is: paying attention to the right things.
—Edward Hall

rational mindscapes

Warren TenHouten, at the University of California at Los Angeles, has been doing some fascinating studies of the language use of the Hopi people. Some of the early results gathered by TenHouten and others indicate that more right-hemisphere activity is present when the Hopi language is used than when English is spoken. Although Hopi language has structure and grammar, it seems to possess several qualities different from English. First, it is nonwritten. That is, Hopi is a spoken language much like the original languages of nearly all Native American cultures. Sign language and the picture-writing common in history are quite different in how they are processed by the brain than are the symbolic-phonetic abstractions we call letters. Because these nonphonetic, nonabstract qualities are so inherent in their communication, Hopi and other Native American languages seem to appeal to the "appositional" or right hemisphere — in our context, the metaphoric mind.

44

The Hopi talk about what they see. The language is constructed in such a way that nature is always the reference when speech is taking place. They focus upon the realities accessible through the senses. When they discuss abstractions, these abstractions are part of the universe of nature. For example, if a Hopi and an English-speaking person were watching a person running across a field, both might say, "He is running;" thus both would be operating from a direct observational basis. Both would be linked to nature. Later on, however, when the runner was gone, it would be appropriate for the English-speaking person to say "He ran away." The Hopi would say something like, "He runs in my memory."

The distinction I hope to draw here is to explore the link between the cyclical and the linear, the rational and the metaphoric, and the perceptions of cultural and natural as manifested in language and language use. Consider the following statement by TenHouten and Kaplan:

> In English, knowledge is rooted in abstraction: That is, the source of knowledge is found in propositions that take space and time to be fundamental. While the Hopi language begins in nature, proceeds to the cultural order, and then leads the speaker back into nature, the English language may do the reverse. In English the journey is such that the logic of English-speaking begins in culture (with propositions, hypotheses, questions and topics) and detours to nature to find empirical proof of the correspondence of such linguistic constructs, only to return once again to culture with a more developed way of speaking. *

* TenHouten, Warren D., and Charles D. Kaplan. *Science and Its Mirror Image.* Harper and Row Publishers, New York, 1973, p. 100.

The real distinction here is not between English and Hopi as languages, but rather in how language affects mind function. If, as is the case with nature-dominated thought, one language starts in nature, moves to the cultural order, and then returns to the natural, it is more cyclical in preference; it is more metaphoric in intent. Thus it becomes more likely that it will nurture the function of the metaphoric mind more easily than it nurtures the abstract linearities of the rational mind. If, on the other hand, the language has a built-in bias toward abstraction, toward linear time, and toward the cultural order, it is more likely that the rational mind will be favored.

Nature is *used* in rational, abstract systems. To paraphrase TenHouten and Kaplan, rationally-dominant languages start with abstractions and nature is referred to only in regard to these abstractions. For example, researchers most often start with an hypothesis or an idea about something. From this starting point, they usually set up a way to "test" nature to see if the hypothesis is correct. Once they complete their testing, they judge the natural events or conditions in terms of the hypothesis. The final result is usually reported as a cultural abstraction about the hypothesis. If such researchers claimed that gravity controls the behavior of falling objects, they could easily go into nature, test, retest, and search about to find evidence for whether or not the natural world behaves as if gravity exists. At the end of such research, the results would undoubtedly be reported in terms of *gravity* rather than of *nature* — in terms, that is, of a cultural rather than a natural explanation.

This pattern of inquiry and logic is the basic premise for nearly all psychological research. As such, it is primarily consistent with the logical philosophy of our culture. It is in line with the thrust of educational, religious, and industrial approaches. It is consistent with the linear, time-ordered ethic of Western thought. The mind function of such inquiry is far more closely allied to what have been identified as the functions of the left cerebral hemisphere than to those of the right cerebral hemisphere.

Thus, with the left-hemisphere dominance of our culture and with our language so powerfully prejudiced toward linear time and logical sequences, it is not surprising that the metaphoric mind is suppressed. Holistic thought, cyclical perceptions, and extended networks of relationships all lack the logical, linear precision so compatible with the rationality of Western bias. Specificity is the virtue, ambiguity the vice. Specificity is the mortar of logic; ambiguity the matrix of metaphor. Thus, our patterns and habits of language use prejudice our thoughts toward the rational-linear.

Let's review the ideas called forth so far in our odyssey of mind:

The child in utero is in natural systems.
The child once born is in cultural systems.
The dominant time mode of natural systems is cyclic.
The dominant time mode of our culture is linear.
Humankind preferred cyclic time until about 10,000 years ago.
Humankind (at least the dominant cultures on earth) now prefer linear time.
Language use reflects the time-mode preference: cyclical for the Hopi and linear for speakers of English.

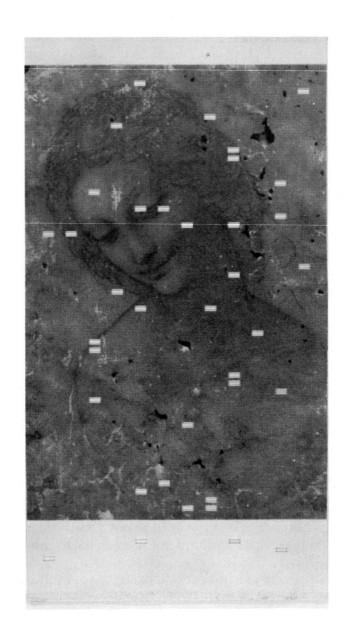

49

Linearity and convergence, as we have noted, have found their way into psychology. Nowhere is this better illustrated than with the behaviorists, whose chosen mode of interpretation resembles the digital computer. ON-OFF . . . STIMULUS-RESPONSE. That's all there was to human learning and human knowledge. Even today there are essentially two kinds of psychologists: those whose methods belie a preference for rationality and linearity, and those who prefer metaphor and cyclic involvement. Generally these foci are separated as scientific psychology and therapeutic psychology. The scientists on one hand, the muses on the other. In our culture the scientist rules over the muse.

The most influential psychologist in America isn't in America at all. He is in Geneva, Switzerland. He was trained as a scientist and has a strong preference for logic and philosophy in his foundations of perception. And as a cult figure he dominates the American educational and psychological arena to an extent matched only by Freud's past and Jung's more recent influence in psychoanalytic circles. He is Jean Piaget.

Piaget functioned intuitively, metaphorically, and with profound holism as he created a rational, logical structure defining and delimiting stages of intellectual growth. In effect the bulk of his profoundly insightful hierarchy of development came from the observation of his own children. He was the Charles Darwin of psychology. He went to nature, looked it full in the face, and painstakingly and intuitively described what he saw. Like Darwin, he saw evolution. Evolution of the individual through stages of involvement with the whole of natural and cultural ecologies.

Piaget's work lay fallow upon the shelves of psychology since the early 1930s with little significant attention paid until recently. So he was, in a way, a contemporary of John Dewey. In his 1933 work, *Logic: A Theory of Inquiry*, Dewey wrote about the analysis of a complete act of linear thought. His work came to be known as a fundamental statement in linear logic. His followers called it The Scientific Method. In psychological terms, Piaget mapped out a similar series of sequential steps in the child's assimilation of logic that his followers hoisted as the banner of total mental development. This four-stage process of Piaget's, in highly condensed form, is outlined next. (Read it from the bottom.)

PRE-OPERATIONAL (2-5 years) This stage is marked by the children's ability to operate on abstractions. That is, they cease being wholly dependent upon what is happening immediately in their environment. They imitate behaviors that happened a long time before, and they visibly begin to demonstrate that they think about things before they do them. In this stage children begin to use language. They use words in sentences during this stage. All in all the child exhibits an ability to begin thinking in abstractions or, as it is called by Piaget, representational thinking. Thought is generally egocentric even though it is abstract; the child's *own* viewpoint seems to dominate and he or she cannot think from another's viewpoint.

SENSORIMOTOR (birth-2 years) The stage at which action takes place with little or no understanding. Early in this stage it is presumed that the child believes that things exist only if they are touched, seen, or heard. If an object is shown to a child and then screened off with a barrier, the child behaves as though the object is gone. When this stage is almost over, children will behave as though they know the object still exists and is only hidden by the barrier. In other words, the child's knowledge is linked specifically to reality of perception. They do not yet do abstract thinking.

FORMAL OPERATIONS (12 years on) Just as concrete operations are characterized by children's being able to limit variables in thought to abstractions, this stage is characterized by their being able to act on two or more abstractions simultaneously. This means that the child thinks logically about one event (such as balancing two people on a teeter-totter) and comes to resolution about it — and simultaneously considers the effects of another logical abstraction on the process. This would be like first resolving that two children could balance on the teeter-totter and then adding the third child in a special place to maintain the balance. It is a stage of sophisticated logic.

CONCRETE OPERATIONAL (5-12 years) Now children are well on the way to becoming abstract logical thinkers. They can speculate about certain events in the physical environment in such a way that they do not need to experience them through the senses to determine the results. In other words, they substitute mental activity for actual sensory experience. At this time children begin to learn to classify elements of the world. That is, they sort objects into classes that separate them from other classes. Children in this stage have formed certain "laws" of logic. If something happens in opposition to the logic, they presume the event is at fault and *not* the logic.

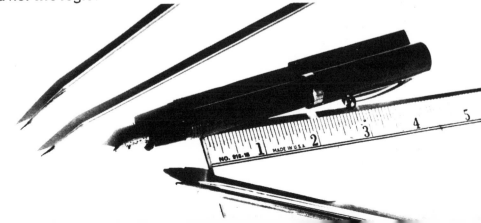

Piaget's work has all but consumed psychologists in colleges and universities for nearly a decade. The logic of his stages seems immutable. Graduate students have earned hundreds of advanced degrees by verifying the validity of each of these stages. For a while Jerome Bruner, mentioned earlier, created a stir by demonstrating that the ages at which children could perform these tasks were not as rigidly defined as Piaget had claimed. He and other psychologists said the process could be speeded up. That is, children could be taught to progress through the stages faster. Piaget seemed unperturbed and effectively answered, "It doesn't matter."

The episode of crying, "Let's speed it up" on this side of the Atlantic and the cool, "It doesn't matter" on the far side clearly typified the whole mentality of two similar but slightly different cultural settings. The popularity of Piaget's stages is obvious — it's logic *about* logic. Thus it has remarkable appeal to intellectuals. The statement by Bruner that the stages could be reached more quickly had great appeal to technocratic managers. After all, if they could measure the *distance* between two things and how *fast* they could move from one place to another, then rationality would reign supreme. Not strangely, in this context these two qualities, distance and rate, were both related to *linear time*.

Piaget's ideas were formulated decades before their popularity. Brilliant though they were, they had little appeal until the 1960s and the Sputnik-spurred explosion to excel. Excel meant, "Regain the advantage over Russian technological supremacy." U.S. embarrassment was real. Technology had been the medium of the violation of the Mother, Flag, and Spaceship ethic. Educators were desperate. The dollar dams had burst, and to qualify for part of the largess they had to play the game of decimal-placed virtue . . . accountability. All of this became woven into a technocratic tapestry as federal money became available. The new sources of money had to be doled out to "responsible" educators. They needed a theory that could be judged. Piaget's fit the bill. Logic affords integer-like specificity. According to the game plan of tidy thinking logic could produce predictable, evaluatable, and countable results. Thus they were accountable. Piaget's bias toward the development of logical consistency and the maturity of rational processes suddenly became the lesson plan for education. Colleges crowded with students from the World War II baby boom mass-produced educators. The new emphasis on excellence in teaching resulted in elaborately expanded departments of teacher training in many colleges and universities. Psychology departments were pressured to put aside their pigeons, cats, and rats to get in on the federal dollars. If they refused, the Educational Psychology department in the next building swelled with new appointments and new energy.

But the content was lacking. A massive educational-guidelines conference of blue-ribbon scientists and educational elite was held in Woods Hole, Massachusetts in 1958. Jerome Bruner, who guided the government's involvement through the fateful Woods Hole conference, was the mentor. And that school of thought which he mented was authored by Piaget. Piaget came off the shelves at Woods Hole. He was the perfect psychological answer to the technocratic data-crazed accountants. The pristine behaviorists couldn't give up their pigeons and rats and so would have to wait to qualify.

Thus it was that accountability brought cognitive and intellectual maturation to the cutting edge of philosophical and psychological concern. The mentality of engineering prevailed. Piaget's models were it.

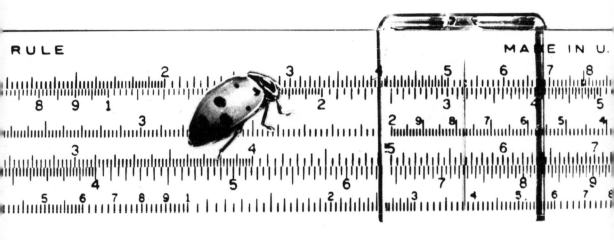

Now let's look again at Piaget's stages. First, they are determined by considering the logical qualities of linear time, space, and language. The medium through which progress is assessed is first behavior without language and later behavior with language. The major criteria of growth are based on progression through a system of logic. Moreover, the behaviors that are observed are filtered through thought patterns dominated by the linear, logical, time-space biases of the observer. *In other words, the assessment of a human's mental or intellectual maturity in the linear schema of Piaget is a circular argument.* If the logic is linear and the observer is trained in linear thinking, there is little chance that the observer can see any maturity developing unless it is growth in linearity. One cannot expect oranges if one plants apples.

This should not be considered harsh criticism against Piaget. All scientific or linear reasoning is biased by the same condition. Following the historical lead of the early Greeks, the Renaissance thinkers created contexts of Western rational thought that resulted in an explosion of scientific insight leading directly to the technical supremacy of modern times. That rationality works isn't the issue . . . *but that it is circular.* Rational thought is its own gift to the world . . . *it presumes that linearity is real while knowing it is not.*

55

Attempting excursion into the metaphoric mind is not an attempt to discredit the rational mind. Without rationality, how could the excursion be made? These words, these sentences, are all images of a rational reality that we share. To this point, the journey has only served to create awareness that there are world views which contradict the notions we have almost habitually come to accept as immutable. Language *does* affect perception and thought. And a culture such as ours, which so systematically teaches us the importance of language, simultaneously creates the values and prejudices embodied within that language.

Piaget, following in the formidable footsteps of Socrates, Aristotle, Newton, and Galileo has put forth a perspective in psychology that is consistent both with the version of Western language called English, and with the linear preferences of Western society in general. Language is both the *tool* and the *weapon* a culture chooses to sculpt and constrain its own image. Since the language is linear and logical and uses nature only as a mechanism to verify its cultural premise, why should Piaget's impact be so surprising? He in fact may have been guilty of only one circularity. He chose logic as the gauge by which he would assess the growth of the intellect. Then he chose language as the medium through which progress toward logic was demonstrated. Thus with a philosophy of linearity (logic) and a process of linearity (language), it is hardly surprising that psychological effectiveness (maturity) was judged by how linear a person was.

The real charade came later, but not with Piaget's Darwinian-like observations of his own children and a surprisingly small group of others which resulted in his model of the stages of intellectual growth. The hundreds of psychologists, graduate students, and anxious educators who grabbed Piaget's cultural order statement and "returned to nature" to reaffirm the cultural order took Piaget's stages, gathered gaggles of children together, and viewed them through the bias of cultural glasses, ending up with nothing more than a stronger prejudice that the cultural-order statement was right.

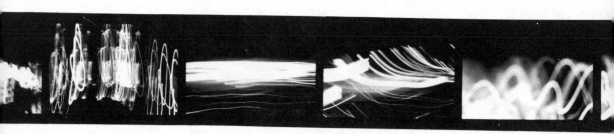

Why should this be so problematical? Simply in this — our culture is so biased toward linearities and rational abstraction that it compulsively carries out the process just described. It verifies the cultural order with nature over and over again. Nature no longer becomes the source of the cultural order; it becomes the laboratory of it.

Who is nature in this strange cultural game? You are . . . I am. All of those of us who are measured, judged, and ranked. Each of us whose life is assessed by the curators of logic. They look at us all through a small opening in human experience. Their limited meter stick measures a small bit of the total capacity of human beings. All the children in schools are meadowlands for these measurers. So too are those gray, quiet humans who sit quietly and watch the same linear clocks that acknowledged their birth tick out the fading final seconds of their lives.

The reason for challenging the rational, linear, culturally ordered constructs that now define the human mind is that in reality they are a half-minded portrait at best. *Piaget's constructs describe only the functions of the left cerebral hemisphere in most humans!*

In no way are these words intended to denigrate the intuitive or the rational genius of Piaget, but rather to criticize the vivid use to which a rationally dominant culture puts such work. Some psychologists, such as Lawrence Kohlberg at Harvard, say Piaget's constructs are so viable that they relate to moral growth. Kohlberg's work is little more than a shift in content that confirms Piaget's hierarchical stages. Kohlberg substitutes abstract moral questions for the abstract logical questions that characterize Piaget's tasks. His stages of moral growth include six stages paralleling Piaget's four. His conclusions are painfully predictable. Children who are adept at abstract manipulation of linear physical concepts are also adept at the abstract manipulation of linear moral concepts. Kohlberg, it appears, further fails to recognize that the bias toward moral linearity is as culturally effected as is a bias toward physical linearity. Logic is its own reward; it creates internal consistency regardless of content.

The pity of this is that Kohlberg maintains that humans cannot be morally operative unless they are at the formal operations stage of Piaget. Culturally this would probably exclude all Hopi, Zuni, Swahili, Maori and Eskimos. The basis for this exclusion would be technical rather than theoretical. Each of these cultures has no formal abstract symbolic language. Thus their cultures do not create a mechanism for them to practice abstract reasoning and therefore score well on the tests of Kohlberg or Piaget. Theoretically neither Piaget nor Kohlberg could allow this condition to be considered moral — theorists must somehow be accountable to those excluded by their theories as well as those included.

The metaphoric mind includes rationality, linearity, and logic — for it created them. But like some children, the rational mind often seems embarrassed by the presence of its parents.

Certainly, the growing seed is gathering nourishment from its environment, but the process is no mere sticking together of the nutritive elements, for it absorbs and transforms them, and one sees nothing like this in the manufacture of an electric motor or computer.

—Alan Watts

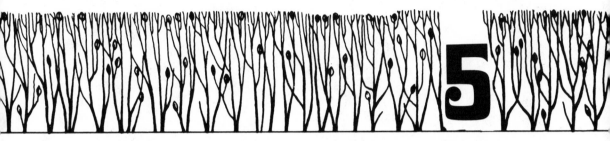

5
shadows of equilibrium

The metaphoric mind is the natural mind. Its functions are enriched but never dominated by the cultural order. It wanders through awarenesses, experiences, images, and all our tacit knowings like a gentle predator as it searches for being. If there are gaps in experience or knowledge, it hardly pauses but seeks an alternative route. If there is no valid alternative route, the metaphoric mind invents one. For that is what it does best . . . it invents.

This quality — invention — is what led Einstein and others to view the intuitive qualities of the metaphoric mind as a "sacred gift." It is enriched by an infinity of knowings, and it ceaselessly repatterns these to a compound infinity of possibilities as it wanders across the face of the world. It creates poems, equations, cities, and universes where none has existed before. In all its knowing, it seems only to lack one thing . . . the knowing that something is impossible.

The courage of the metaphoric mind is built on a base of acceptance. Like its ancestor, the natural world, the metaphoric mind has none of the limiting qualities of the cultural order. It has no competition; it has only the slightest hints of aggression and these are related to survival; it has no capacity to evaluate and judge. It is natural. It is this mind that sees itself as one with all. It cannot perceive itself apart from other entities. It is the mind that nontechnical cultures often see as the mind of all . . . of sky, of rock, of sea, and of all living things. It is the mind that knows. Sometimes one thing uses another, like the lion and the zebra, but there is no question of right or wrong or competition. This is simply the way things are.

It is not a mind without compassion nor in fact without structure. It is the mind that invented compassion, and its structure is designed to exhibit processes that are inclusive and expanding. At some time in Marshack's "distant past," humans achieved complexity in their awareness of their ability to be *from* nature rather than *of* nature. Humans began to know they could *take energy* from the natural world

Perhaps this act of *taking* energy was the original sin. Taking is the act of the aggressor, the rapist, the conqueror. It is the act of those who set themselves apart from nature. Humans in equilibrium with nature *accepted* energy. They never took more than was needed. They changed little, for they did not interrupt the natural cycles. But the humans who *did* take energy — who interrupted the cycles — became dedicated to controlling nature. They changed the setting. They could grow more than they needed . . . and thus allow more humans to appear.

As the numbers of people grew and the matrix of communication expanded, language became refined. With that refinement came the knowing that the metaphoric mind could not be translated into the technology of language and new-found ability to exploit natural energy. A simpler, more manageable way had to be found. The rational mind was invented.

It was tidy, but thought not to be tidy enough, so the gathered swarms of people set about making it more so. Because communication is a game played in public, there must be rules. Consensus became a strategy. After all, there could not be six or seven words for one object. The most refined players of the game came up with *one* word. Grammar was next. The rules of discourse should reflect the logic of the labeling. Gradually the acts of discussing things in the past and in the future crept into regular conversations, reflecting a "knowing" and adaptive ability on the part of the metaphoric mind. With this invention of the metaphoric mind, the rational mind became jolted into accommodation, so it began thinking in forms of logic that were terse abstractions of what the metaphoric mind knew. It referred logically to future and to past. Tenses were created. New rules were formed, with each new rule specifying conformity and excluding alternatives in the structure. No one knows when or where it happened. Maybe it was in Sumeria . . . perhaps the Indus Valley or in some culture not yet discovered . . . but the wondrous, wandering ways of the metaphoric mind performed a frightening act of submission. They accepted the dominance of the rational mind.

The rule-making and game-playing mind wrote its own declaration of independence. Oh, it knew it wasn't independent, but it did write the rules as though it were. At the same time, the original sin continued. More energy was taken. Soon animals, trees, rocks, and precious metals all became victim to the not-so-gentle predation of the rational mind.

Unlike its parents, the rational mind exploited. It learned to do so whenever its rules came in contact with rules created by other humans. To resolve this conflict, the rational mind invented competition. Sometimes competition was restricted to the arena of logic, but more often it became physical. Cultural orders were not satisfied to attack nature as they took energy but soon adopted the exploitation of other cultural orders. Now it was complete. The metaphoric mind had dropped into the prison created by its child. But it never languished into death. It could not be destroyed . . . only suppressed.

We may now have gone full cycle. Today our culture is beginning to question the imprisonment of the metaphoric mind. Its natural manifestations of day and night dreaming, of fantasy, and of guided imagery are all subjects of renewed interest. Expanded and altered consciousness may well be misnomers for returning to the more natural states of the metaphoric mind. Drugs, yoga, meditation, hypnosis, and repetitive movement may all be access routes in the form of currently

popular "visitation rituals" to those imprisoned capacities that we once used freely.

Strangely enough, the powers of the rational mind are now being vigorously applied to research that seeks to map and legitimize the existence of the metaphoric mind. Perhaps the child has developed a guilty conscience about the parent. Such guilt is probably intrinsic: each human is probably aware that both minds function within us and that we have overindulged one at the expense of the other. But the more likely reason for our getting infatuated with the metaphoric mind is that the cultural order of the world is in trouble.

Population has exploded. The original sin of energy taken is exacting its toll. Energy suppliers are now making changes in the cultural order of energy users. Natural systems are becoming more remote to the experience of most human beings and the sense of alienation is almost overwhelming.

Alienation of cultures from each other . . . of humans from culture . . . of humans from each other . . . and, perhaps most importantly, of humans from nature — all these are symptoms of the abandonment to prison of the metaphoric mind by the rational mind. If there is to be survival, the realms of nature, its cyclic time, its metaphoric reservoirs, and its mind in humans must be resurrected. The sacred gift must be brought back into harmony with the faithful servant.

Disequilibrium always creates action in natural systems. Seldom is resolution of disequilibrium complete, but there is always a tendency toward harmony. Low-pressure systems in the atmosphere appear and air rushes into their centers from areas of higher pressure. When gravitational pull exceeds the inertia of rocks on a mountainside, they fall. When too many foxes appear, the relative numbers of rabbits drop. It is unlikely that the human minds function differently, even in the face of cultural oppression. When the metaphoric mind dominated, it used its freedom to invent the rational mind. *Now that the rational mind appears to dominate, it is creating access routes to the metaphoric mind.* Perhaps contemporary interest, modern research, the thousands of seminar-workshops springing up all over the nation, and even this book are no more than steps in the progress of this disequilibrium toward harmonious resolution.

> There is something antic about creating although the enterprise be serious.
>
> —Jerome Bruner

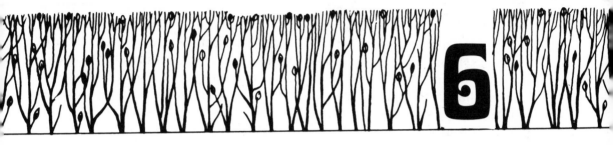

the gift of beginning

Early in the 1960s I was invited to work with some curriculum researchers at Harvard. This work, funded by the National Science Foundation, was intent on producing instructional materials, strategies, and tactics that would relate to the "whole child" in the act of learning science. None of us, the National Science Foundation included, had the ghost of an idea what that meant. As a result, we all juggled our values and prejudices in each other's presence and sought out a kind of eclectic bag of premises to start with. At that gathering Jerome Bruner, David Hawkins, and William Gordon were most influential in affecting my thinking about the metaphoric mind. Bruner, because he used the metaphor of right-handed and left-handed knowing referred to in Chapter Two. Hawkins, because he took great delight in creating complex scientific-experience explanations for what children were *really* experiencing when they did relatively simple things. Gordon, who provided me with the first hints of structure for the metaphoric modes of knowing.

Bruner had written a fine book called *On Knowing, Essays for the Left Hand*, and he introduced me to this metaphor as a basis for observations I would make that summer and the following year. Although both Bruner and Hawkins were disciples of Piaget, neither insisted that Piaget's models be used. Instead we gathered each day, planned some action assignments, tried them with classrooms full of children, discussed them later, and wrote down our findings. Children of all ages were available to us, so we could run the gamut from Piaget's pre-operational to supposedly formal operations stages. Because I felt no compulsion at that time to reverify Piaget's logical progression, I chose to discover what I could about left-handed learning.

One of the first things I learned was that it was more like play than work. The children would take the "problem" we had created and literally play with it. Since our work usually involved some apparatus or some natural materials, the children had something tangible to work on. In a typical beginning, given a series of pendulums hanging from wooden racks, the children were instructed to "Find out what you can about pendulums."

> Children picked up the racks, looked underneath, set them down, and began to swing pendulums. Some started pendulum wars (trying to hit pendulum spheres together). Some chattered about the swings on the playground. Two boys began trying to entwine their pendulum cords by swinging the pendulums. A girl leaned over the frame with her lips on the top, feeling the vibrations as the pendulum swung back and forth. Three boys and one girl tried to make a stack of pendulums so there would be a tower of pendulums that they could get to swing in unison. (This activity took about 40 minutes.)

At first I noticed a good deal of anxiety on the part of the adults who had written the lessons. Most often they would circulate among the students and ask leading questions — questions designed to "lead" the children back to where the adults were more comfortable, to a place where the lesson and experience were more closely related to the intent of the lesson as seen by the adults.

In these instances David Hawkins protected the children as they explored. He would weave great rational tales about the sophistication of some of the children's actions, much to the comfort of those whose rational neurosis was being sorely taxed. He invoked everyone from Galileo to Confucius as he guaranteed a space of time for the children to "mess around" (one of his favorite phrases). Bruner most often agreed and spoke about "left-handed" knowing. I was enraptured by the lack of structure the children showed until the nervous adults crept in and asked questions or otherwise guided their actions back into "safe" places.

Thus I was able to observe children playing with science and simultaneously gather several important psychological insights from those participating:

Bruner: The students were involved in play, rich in "left-handed" knowing.

Hawkins: There were profound rational components being experienced tacitly by the children.

Other adults: Teachers are generally made nervous by play.

Samples: Adults (the cultural order) affect the kind of knowing the children are permitted to experience.

On the basis of these observations I decided to get a group of lesson-makers together. My purpose was to work with children of several ages, in several content areas, and see how they operated through a learning sequence. That is, I chose to observe them until they were really "finished" with a problem. I did not know whether comprehension or boredom would finish the learning. We worked with third graders (7-8 years old), sixth graders (11-12 years old), and eighth graders (13-14 years old). The content areas included physics, natural science, and astronomy. The results were remarkable.

All the students indulged in play for a long period of time at the onset of the lesson. This play was facilitated by the degree of "trust" we had established with the children. They would often cue in on the adults to see how much we intended to interfere before they got comfortable with the play. The older students always took longer to be convinced of our "nonintervention" policy. We mapped the excursions of individual students into play-work areas. Work was defined as that activity with obvious rational components. Play was that which lacked these components. The results of several dozen observations that summer and several hundred in the following year are shown in the illustrations that follow.

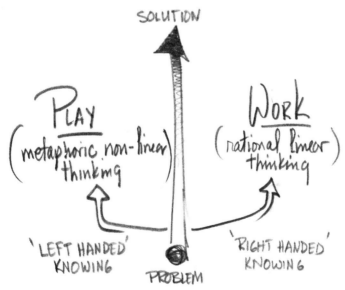

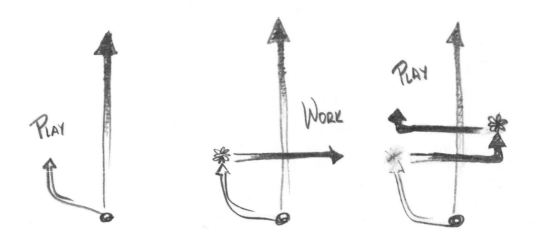

Generally the students would spend most of their early time within a problem sequence in play. Then, as they reached saturation with the play, they would shift to right-handed or rational knowing. At this point the teacher-observers typically became noticeably more comfortable. The children were operating within the context of their prejudices. They asked questions, performed tasks, and generally conformed to behaviors that were consistent with Piaget's criteria.

The students, however, were quickly satiated with rational discourse. They often gathered their newfound data and then whipped back into metaphoric play in the left-handed mode. After exhausting their rational fix in metaphor, however, the students again excursioned into the right. This always delighted the teachers. But they became bewildered again as the students frequently whipped once more into metaphor. I began to realize that the teachers were exhibiting a form of neurosis consistent with the cultural order . . . rational neurosis. *The teachers were made anxious when the children moved away from the structures the teachers had chosen to accept.*

"Metaphoric Play" was difficult to get into at this level.

Students got very solution-oriented. They left metaphor in the problem and sought it in the situation. They looked for non-verbal cues in adults and created logical explanations accordingly.

In total time spent ... more meta-phoric at first ... more rational near the end.

Back and forth the pattern went, with alternating excursions from right to left on the part of the students and into and out of anxiety on the part of the teachers. But gradually it got better for the teachers. We began to notice that about two-thirds of the way through a problem-solution sequence, the right-handed knowing began to dominate. That is, the closer the children got to a rational solution, *the more difficult it was for them to return to metaphor.* This difficulty was demonstrated by the students consistently choosing linear and logical explanations and routes for exploration. Even when led in less logical directions, the students clung tenaciously to their rational conclusions. Additional phenomena became apparent at this point. The students appeared more serious, many lost their smiles, their body movement diminished, and their eye contact increased as they sought visual cues and approval. The students seemed to drop back into low trust patterns.

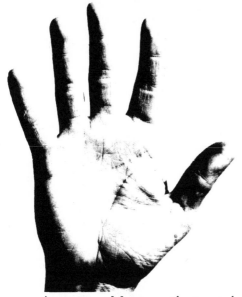

A series of factors that might contribute were explored, among them the notion that the children had picked up on adult anxiety and were trying to reduce that. A second possibility was that the discussions the children had with each other resulted in a consensus posture. A third was that they had in fact rationally solved the problem. A fourth was that they had tired of the experience and had decided to "play the game." It would be unfair not to suggest a fifth alternative, namely that the students actually preferred rational thought. (This option is included in the spirit of rationality . . . however, the therapeutic evidence of the students' tension suggests it is an unlikely possibility.) For the next twelve years I was to pursue this issue.

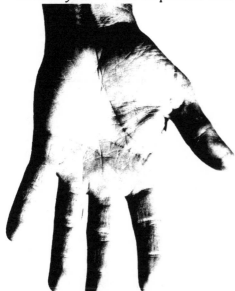

Near the end of the first summer I met and briefly worked with William Gordon, the originator of Synectics. Synectics, an invented word meaning connecting the unconnected, is both a process and a content area. It was the first formal classification of the way the metaphoric mind might function that I had seen. Though it was not Gordon's intent to deal with mind structure, his moving the concept of *metaphor* out of the rational clutches of humanities scholars gave a verbal quality to a here-to-for noun. That construct gave me a rational base with which to explore the metaphoric mind.

Gordon was after creativity. He wanted to develop methods by which humans could disrupt the linear prejudices of thinking and explore more divergently the realm of possible solutions to problems. He used a series of stages of analogic thought patterns. Analogy nurtures a level of ambiguity that carries a problem outside its own ruts. The components of analogic reasoning he chose were Direct, Personal, Symbolic, and Fantasy.

Direct analogy is characterized by direct comparisons between objects, processes, or conditions: clouds and cotton, for example, or the sea and the prairie. Personal analogies are created when the observer physically becomes part of the object, process, or condition: dancing like a tree. Symbolic analogy involves the use of symbols or objective substitutions for objects, processes, or conditions: $F = ma$. Gordon has now abandoned the Fantasy analogy but it originally meant a kind of wish-fulfillment exploration of objects, processes, or conditions such as role-playing.

When I was first introduced to these concepts and linked them to the anxieties shown by educators in the face of left-handed (right hemisphere) thinking on the part of students, I chose to pursue the creation of structural strategies for the metaphoric mind. It was also at this time that I came to realize the bewildering complexity of any attempt to do so. Even now I make no claim that the metaphoric modes are quantitatively or objectively established, though I believe they could be by those so inclined. Instead I see them simply as major arenas of metaphoric functioning. Within each are a myriad of alternatives and combinations. Each moves in and out of focus as do clouds and light in passing through air. Since we are pursuing order in the metaphoric mind we must do so as we would pursue it in nature . . . full of optimism that the order we create will do little harm and full of awareness that this, like any other order, is only transitory. Any theory or premise we impose upon nature is only a quiet eddy in the currents of mind. It is destined to disappear.

Metaphor, far from being a decoration that is added to language, purifies it and restores it to its original nature.

—Claude Levi-Strauss

metaphoric mindscapes

Unlike the hierarchies of intellectual development created by Piaget, the metaphoric modes of thought are *not* naturally hierarchical. They do not depend upon age or chronological maturity for their presence. Their presence is strongly influenced by the cultural order, however. As a result, children often lose the tendency to utilize some of these modes because of pressures from within the rationally dominant culture. This means that by the time they are adults and have conformed to these pressures, they must often be reintroduced to the metaphoric modes of thinking.

With the reintroduction, a hierarchy of access emerges — a pattern created primarily by the culture. The order in which I will present these modes is related to the ease with which these strategies are accepted by adults who function in our society. In other words, I offer first that metaphoric mode which I find to be most acceptable to our rationally dominant culture. The last presented is the most difficult for the adult culture to accept.

82

Adults generally operate in thought styles that reflect the long years they spent growing up in our culture. They have been schooled and trained and have experienced years of communication that have channeled their thought processes into rational ruts. They possess and exaggerate the social skills of rationality to such a degree that it is difficult for them *not* to exercise skills when they think. Executives, teachers, or surgeons will tend to think about problems in ways that reflect their earlier experience. In a sense cultural experience tends to preprogram our thought patterns to respond to problems with the mental skills we used to cope successfully with the same problem the last time we were confronted with it.

Children, on the other hand, do not have such cultural skill banks. As a result they approach each problem in a new way, as though each new task never existed before. They have no ruts, no preprograms, and no stock solutions. This attitude of freshness is responsible for the quality we call "naiveté" in children. It led J. Robert Oppenheimer to remark, "I could solve my most complex problems in physics if I had not given up the ways of thinking common to children at play."

Edward DeBono calls experts those in the deepest ruts worn by repeatedly experiencing the same issues over and over again. He points out that once such "habits" form it requires an incredible amount of energy to struggle out of them. Children without the ruts of expertise use

metaphoric strategies interchangeably. They do not have the habits created by experience, so they invent solutions rather than rehearsing old ones.

Herein lies our age-old social quandary. Experience and maturity do create expertise and mental skills that *could* arm one with vividly useful tools in thought processes. But so too does experience imprison one's thought processes. The tools become compartments, categories, and limiting conditions. Abraham Maslow pointed out that one who has a hammer treats the whole world as if it were a nail. Children may take the same hammer and dig with it, sculpt with it, weigh down papers between which they press leaves, *and/or* use it to knock apples from a tree.

Children thus possess the ability to invent but not to conform. They lack cultural experience so they reinvent the wheel with every excursion into involvement with life. Adults have a rich repertoire of cultural experience but have generally given up the tendency to invent. My approach has been to bring these qualities to equilibrium, presenting the metaphoric modes in the most fruitful sequence by which to reinstate inventiveness in adults. Children exhibit involvement in these modes in almost the reverse order as they mature.

These modes are discussed in the pages that follow. Later in the book, you will find other qualities discussed that serve as access routes to each mode. But first, the descriptions of each.

THE SYMBOLIC METAPHORIC MODE

The symbolic metaphor exists whenever a symbol, *either abstract or visual*, is substituted for some object, process, or condition. Letters of the alphabet, numerals, mathematical symbols, and other technical images comprise the *abstract* category in this mode. Trademarks, some roadsigns, logos, and many map markings are but a few symbols that fit in the *visual* category of this mode. Both categories of symbols have a visual component, but one is processed primarily in the left hemisphere (the abstract) while the other (visual) is more compatible with right-hemisphere functions.

Since the invention of writing, the symbolic mode has been the primary exemplar of the cultural order. It is the metaphoric mode most useful and efficient in keeping records, framing laws, and educating others. It is the metaphoric medium that gave rationality the tools to build its dominance.

Symbolic metaphors are often interchangeable, with several meanings, but the meanings are usually tied to an abstract or visual language. Trademarks and logos, though visual, are intended to substitute for words. However, both visual and abstract symbols tend to have far fewer meanings than the modes to be discussed later.

85

The visual symbolic metaphor is typified by Egyptian pictographs and Native American petroglyphs, and it is more widely in current use as Chinese and Japanese pictographs or ideagraphs. The Japanese counterpart of the original Chinese visual language is called Kanji. The visual symbolic Kanji metaphors are portraits of ideas with no clue as to how they should be pronounced. Thus to learn them one must use the entire image as a holistic cue system which portrays the meaning. The psychological process is similar to the way people recognize a face. They see the whole face and do not concentrate on the parts.

The Kanji symbols are used widely in Japan. The Japanese, however, with their burgeoning technological society, were forced to develop other language forms. These language forms were made up of abstract symbols rather than visual symbols. Their purpose was to make the process of communicating technical and scientific terms more efficient. One of these abstract language forms is called Katakana. It approaches language phonetically. That is, it creates abstract images of sounds. In this way it is far more abstract than Kanji. Much like phonetic approaches in English, the Katakana symbols do not represent things, but the collection of sounds they portray when spoken or read is understood as the label of an object, process, or condition.

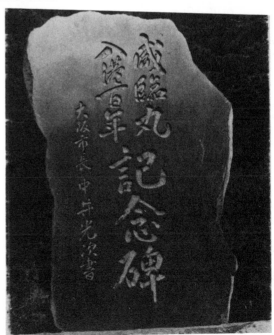

スイヒ口 KATAKANA

Norman Geschwind researched the results of left-hemisphere (rational mind) strokes in both English-speaking and Japanese-speaking people. Like dozens of other researchers, he found an abundance of evidence that left-hemisphere strokes often result in aphasia, a condition in which the ability to read and write is impaired. The unique result reported by Geschwind is that in Japanese-speaking people, left-hemisphere strokes resulted in loss of the ability to read and write *only in the Katakana alphabet*. That is, people suffering left-hemisphere strokes lost the ability to manipulate the logic of the *abstract symbolic alphabet*. They retained the ability to read and write in Kanji, in the visual symbolic realm.

 KANJI

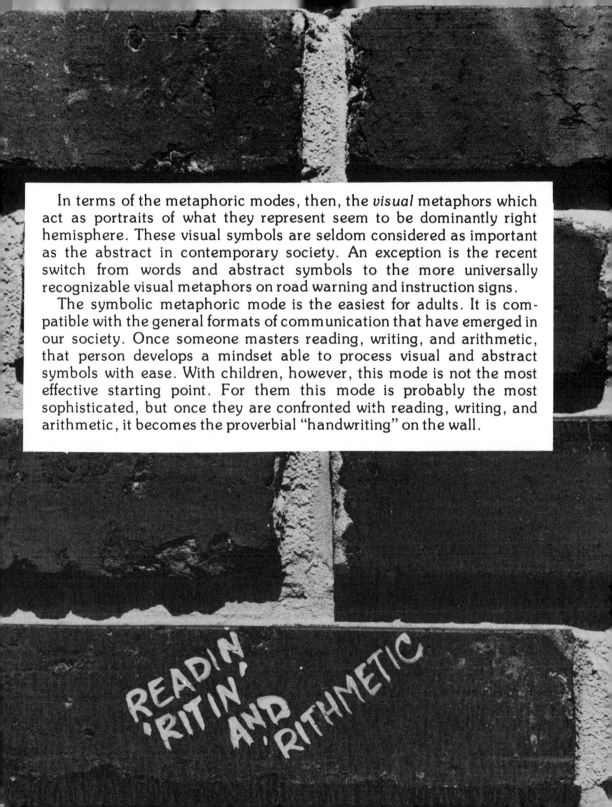

In terms of the metaphoric modes, then, the *visual* metaphors which act as portraits of what they represent seem to be dominantly right hemisphere. These visual symbols are seldom considered as important as the abstract in contemporary society. An exception is the recent switch from words and abstract symbols to the more universally recognizable visual metaphors on road warning and instruction signs.

The symbolic metaphoric mode is the easiest for adults. It is compatible with the general formats of communication that have emerged in our society. Once someone masters reading, writing, and arithmetic, that person develops a mindset able to process visual and abstract symbols with ease. With children, however, this mode is not the most effective starting point. For them this mode is probably the most sophisticated, but once they are confronted with reading, writing, and arithmetic, it becomes the proverbial "handwriting" on the wall.

THE SYNERGIC-COMPARATIVE METAPHORIC MODE

The synergic-comparative mode exists when two or more external objects, processes, or conditions are compared in such a way that both of the external components unite to become more than either one alone because of the comparison. Comparison is a standard strategy of the rational mind. But in standard rational comparisons, the strategy is reductive. Meanings and relationships are delimited and almost surgically separated by the logic of rational mind functions. Not so in metaphor. When comparisons are made in the metaphoric mode, a synergic kind of transformation takes place. Consider for example, Alfred Noyes's famous line from "The Highwayman": "The road was a ribbon of moonlight over the purple moor." The qualities of roadness are combined with the qualities of ribbonness — and both concepts are extended by the union. Of course, a dash of moonlight and purple moor didn't hurt the combination.

The concept of *synergy* is important in all of the functions of the metaphoric mind. Synergy exists when all the parts of a system work together so that their effect is greater than the sum effect of the parts working independently. In a symbolic abstract mode statement this kind of synergic comparison could be suggested by writing $2 + 2 = 5$.

Synergic-comparative metaphors always extend the network of possibilities in thinking. The mind functioning in the synergic-comparative mode discovers relationships in situations external to itself. Externality to self is the key to the difference between this mode and the next to be discussed . . . the integrative mode.

After the highly objective symbolic mode metaphors, the synergic-comparative mode metaphors are most objective. This is because the person using this mode remains *outside* the objects, processes, or conditions that are being compared. The person is reasonably detached and only through the act of bringing the qualities of these externals together is the insight toward their extension of meanings realized. Noyes remained outside the road and the ribbon but transformed both by linking them.

The synergic-comparative metaphoric mode is fairly safe culturally. Although scientists and other supposedly objective rational people are often criticized for using metaphors, they usually do so in their speaking while surgically removing them from their writing. However, those who avoid metaphoric thinking in science almost always give up a chance at the kind of creative insight that usually figures in achievements worthy of a Nobel prize.

Synergic-comparative metaphors abound in literature, science, and everyday conversation. The Volkswagen "bug" or "beetle" is an example. Many people who think of their automobiles as organisms name them and develop attachments that transcend the human-machine relationship. Unfortunately most users of synergic-comparative metaphors stop with the labeling . . . another trick of the rational mind. Instead of comparing "insectness" and "automobileness," they tend to stop as soon as the VW/bug link is made. During and after World War II, air force officials were astounded at the incredible ease with which Eskimos became skilled maintenance workers on sophisticated aircraft. As their acuity was examined, it became obvious that the Eskimos thought of the aircraft as being alive. They acknowledged circulatory systems, nervous systems, and all the rest. The Eskimos approached their work in a mystical reverie about the objects to which they ministered their "healing."

Technical specialists are made nervous by all metaphors, but none make them more nervous than products of the comparative mode. To refer to excretory systems as "body plumbing" and to aircraft airfoil surfaces as "wings" drives some of the more neurotic rational specialists up a wall. Particularly annoying to these types are anthropomorphic tendencies . . . the assignment of human qualities to nonhuman things. "Weeping willow," "clannish birches," and "rocks standing in the agony of rejection" do not bother some people much, but compulsively rational scientists may become furious when someone suggests that "these plants *want* to grow here" or "how those canyon walls protect that stream." The source of annoyance to the scientist is subtle but deeply ingrained. The rational mind is all too aware that all knowledge is metaphor. Any idea, classification, or label that the human mind creates in the name of rationality or objectivity is anthropomorphic. Again the rational mind is threatened by its parent. When the human mind returns to nature and pretends objectivity, it is no wonder that nature metaphorically smiles back.

THE INTEGRATIVE METAPHORIC MODE

The integrative metaphoric mode occurs when the physical and psychic attributes of the person involved are extended into direct experience with objects, processes, and conditions outside themselves. This mode requires "getting into it." One's entire body — mind, emotions, sexuality — is called into play. If criticism can be leveled at the synergic-comparative metaphoric mode for the heresy of its anthropomorphism, then the integrative mode is the supreme sacrilege. It *requires* anthropomorphism. It is a celebration of the total energy of the human experiencing it to transcend the containers we have created with our minds and bodies . . . and it is a total re-entry into the mainstream of nature. In it I *am* nature and whatever part of it I approach is part of me. I move as a tree because I am a tree . . . I think as I do about trees because they are me.

Many nontechnical cultures seem to have large portions of their knowing linked to this metaphoric mode. Carlos Castaneda recently popularized this mode of knowing in the Don Juan series, a quartet of books in which the "knowledge" of a Yaqui shaman was explored. The Yaqui way of knowing provides a lucid and cogent insight into the integrative metaphoric mode. It also explores the conflict between this mode and rational consciousness.

Claude Levi-Strauss, in his many accounts of nontechnical cultures, cites the mysticism or mystical awareness with which so many of these cultural groups approach nature. Speaking from a more technical culture, none can exceed the affection which Albert Einstein had for this mode of knowing . . . "the most beautiful and profound emotion one can feel is a sense of the mystical . . . it is the dower of all true science."

The mysticism of which modern humans speak when they affiliate with this metaphoric mode may in reality be a statement of sensory nostalgia. Children and infants seem deeply involved in the integrative mode nearly all the time. They do not restrict their sensory involvement to the aloof detachment that marks adultness — looking and poking. Instead they often dive headlong into involvement. They immerse themselves in total sensory absorption of the issue. Touching, tasting, mimicking, moving, dancing, and acting out the living and dying of whatever object, process, or condition they are confronted with is only natural. Sometimes their sensory involvement means a suppression of the major senses similar to meditative states. Meditative states in children are guised in the form of the trance-inducing chants they often repeat over and over, and in the repeated body rhythms that seem to go on endlessly in the presence of exasperated adults. Day dreams are also a common form of child-meditation.

It is this unabashed acceptance — allowing all the identifiable and some nonidentifiable senses freedom to be present — that led Einstein, as he explored the stratosphere of physical knowledge, to remark that most scientific advances involved a childlike joy. He and others said real discoveries were made because they reinstated ways of sensing that most had given up long ago. Most of Einstein's metaphors were metaphors of motion that involved the human body's sensing changes in physical conditions.

Researchers who study the human body and its ability to sense input from the environment are becoming convinced that the cliche of there being five senses is absurd. Even adding the token "sixth" sense is platitudinous. Evidence is mounting that we probably possess *twenty* or more senses. Some humans clearly detect minute changes in gravitational and magnetic fields. Others can detect the energy created by a flow of material in pipes, movement through soil, or electrostatic currents in the air. As adults such people are considered unique, mystical, or deviant in some other way. It may well be that these people have simply retained an awareness of senses they possessed as children. Thus when citing the "loss" of these abilities, the majority of adults may be indulging in the sensory nostalgia I spoke of.

One characteristic of the integrative mode is that it tends to get people into much higher and more sophisticated awareness levels than any rational mode accomplishes. The reason is simple. Rational modes invite people to get bogged down in definitions. Recently at a workshop in metaphoric development, one of my colleagues asked a group of Ph.D. specialists in the social and political sciences to demonstrate nonverbally the concept of political efficacy. As the shyness wore off, some very sophisticated scholars began, in a frightening kind of silence, manipulating people into preferred groups. They used a variety of techniques that included coercion, force, ridicule, exclusion, and bribe. It was all good fun and we finally stopped amid laughter and good-hearted exchanges.

However, when I asked some of the children who were bystanders to this activity what had been demonstrated, they told us in political, physical, and psychological terms of such sophistication that the scholars looked bewilderedly at each other. One said, "Oh yeh . . . what those guys were doing was to get all those people to do what they wanted whether the people wanted to do it or not . . ." Another, "Man, they used every trick in the book . . . coaxing, grabbing, bribing, and even pretending to be nice. They changed their ways too . . . When that one guy started getting too many of the people then this other guy changed his style to get some of them back . . . and some folks could never get it together at all!" And finally, "The trick is to know what the people want and then give them enough so you can get what you want." The children ranged from nine to thirteen and had never heard the phrase "political efficacy" before.

Thus when Jerome Bruner said, to the chagrin of many of his psychological colleagues, that any subject could be taught at any level with some degree of intellectual honesty . . . he was right. It is just that the rational neurosis that has clutched the soul of education for the last ten decades cannot see beyond its own fragile expertise into the realms of metaphor.

THE INVENTIVE METAPHORIC MODE

The inventive metaphoric mode is in action whenever a person creates a new level of awareness of knowing as the result of self-initiated exploration of objects, processes, or conditions. The word *creates* is the key. Once when commenting upon Isaac Newton's statement that "the purpose of the scientist is to sail the oceans of the unknown and discover the islands of truth," Bruner impetuously burst forth with the claim, "Nonsense — the purpose of the scientist is to sail the oceans of the unknown and INVENT the islands of truth."

By definition the inventive mode requires invention. But invention is a private activity. Not that it cannot be done in public or with the help of others, but rather that the personal knowing one has invented . . . creates a new status of affiliation with the universe which is very private. This privacy is often discredited when it goes public. For example, I once saw a teenage boy who had become infatuated with cooking spend several weeks doing things with rice. He added bouillon to the cooking water, sprinkled different kinds of herbs on it, and even "buttered" it with peanut butter once. At every juncture he was greeted with the jovial kind of ridicule all too many families regard as an expression of love. The ridicule was complete when his culminating rice dish was shown clearly to be identical to a well-known recipe, but without the shrimp!

This young man and many others are taught by such experiences not to express themselves in inventive ways. Because mental myopia persuades us that personal invention and public invention must be the same, every child is supposed to surpass the Mona Lisa with the first crayon. If not, the work is "nice," but certainly not inventive. The inventive mode *may* be public . . . but it *must* be private.

This metaphoric mode is perhaps the most dynamic of the four, because it is so incredibly all-inclusive. In some ways it is as unfair to refer to it as "metaphoric" as to call it rational. When the inventive qualities of the metaphoric mind are operative, *all* the formal and informal knowings of both the left and right cerebral hemispheres are engaged. Convergence, divergence, and non-vergence occur at once and none dominates. The mind gathers valid linearities and casts them into cyclic metaphoric thinking to seek out where they belong. They tumble and churn and, like magnets tossed into a whirlpool, gradually form patterns of meaning. If these patterns are *valid*, they are retained. If not, they are lost and there is no sense of regret or remorse. The patterns of meaning can be in any medium. Mathematics, words, art, emotion, color, movement, and all the others are viable and legitimate.

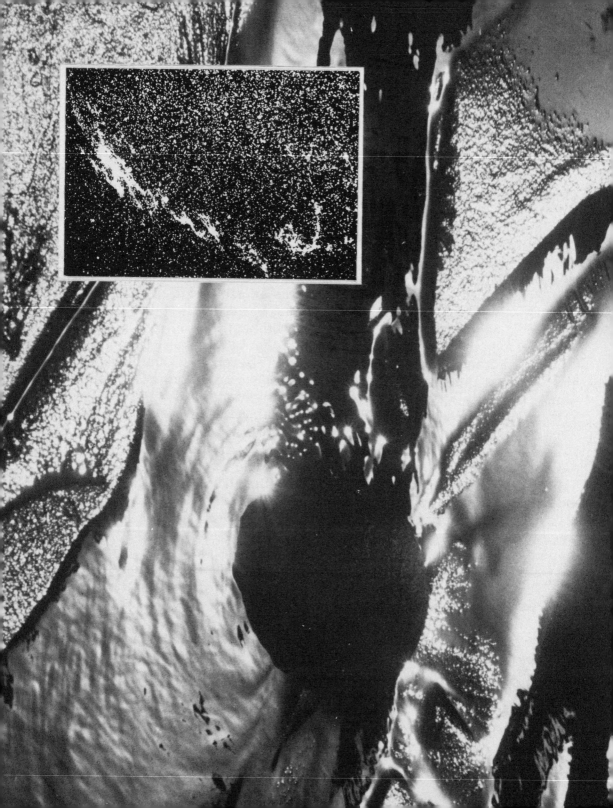

When the inventive mode is functioning, a total synergic kind of knowing evolves. Exploration has the quality of a dream. Objects, processes, and conditions emerge, merge, and dissolve with no reason. The configurations that last do so because they have personal meaning, but not necessarily a public reason. Great courage is required at this stage because ego is transcended. Psychological fragilities are forgotten and they impose no retarding influence on the freedom of exploration. The total energies of intellectuality, emotionality, and sexuality merge into a force at once passive and aggressive. There is resolution to be, but not to control. The euphoria of discovery provides a continuing, peaceful orgasm of pan-existence. Giving and taking, dismissing and possessing all become the same. In this state of viable openness the invention, the creation, the peak experience . . . happens.

That that invention or creation has figured before in human history is of no consequence. The person submitted fully to the maelstrom of experience that is the metaphoric mode and *had the courage to remain.* It matters little if someone else wrote *that* poem, painted *that* painting, or cooked *that* recipe . . . it only matters that *you* did or *I* did.

The inventive mode is the natural mind. It is the blend of parent and child. It is the peak human condition as it involves total participation in the whole of the natural scheme. It is the gift of three billion years and is not likely to remain suppressed in the face of its lesser inventions. Jonas Salk comments upon this synergic mode as follows:

The artist draws largely upon that part of the mind that functions beneath consciousness . . . while the scientist by and large, but not exclusively, uses that part of the mind that functions in consciousness. The part of the mind that functions beneath consciousness also operates during consciousness . . . It is necessary to learn how to draw more upon it and employ it for solving the problems of life, of survival, and of evolution. Wisdom arises from both parts of the mind.

*Salk, Jonas. *The Survival of the Wisest.* Harper and Row Publishers, New York, 1973.

As nature continues its game of biological mutation and selection, and as Man plays his own games of selection of ideas and of cultural innovations, Nature will have the last word.

—Jonas Salk

8

a short editorial

Jean Piaget once wrote that learning a concept takes place only to the degree to which it is reinvented. I mention this to make it clear that the overemphasis on tacit linearities earlier pages may have implied in his hierarchies does not represent the whole of Piaget's posture. However, Piaget *has* said on other occasions that his preferred interest is in the logical workings of the mind and not on the capricious world of the subconscious. Thus the fragmentary dichotomy that humankind has created is nurtured by Piaget and supported by our contemporary society. My friend Richard Barnhart once created a poster with the slogan:

> If I criticize others for re-inventing the wheel
> I am probably more interested in wheels
> . . . than invention

Inherent in Piaget's developmental stages is a steadily growing refinement of convergent logic. This refinement culminates in Formal Operations, highly different from the chaotic, indiscriminate Sensorimotor stage where involvement with every kind of input is common. In the strategies of the metaphoric mind outlined here, there may appear to be an appeal for the opposite process . . . and in some ways there is. This "inversion" effect has some remarkable characteristics, including both similarities and differences when compared to Piaget.

The Sensorimotor repertoire has as its basic quality the quality of invention. Children in the first two years of life are inventing the whole universe that they perceive. Much later will come pressure to assimilate the conformity-laden cultural precedents. From the crib children are totally immersed in sensing all things. The clatter in the kitchen, the warm cooing sounds from parents, the feelings they get from different colors, the warmth, the cold, the feeling of liquids going into their bodies, the feeling of liquids coming out . . . all are of equal importance. Some even suggest that it is not an optical quandary facing children in the first few weeks of birth when they have trouble focusing — it may be a super sensory one. Newborn and early infants probably see the auras of energy associated with our bodies . . . a phenomenon we confuse with their eyes being "out of focus." Such claims of "eye focus" problems are made by adults who lost their ability to see auras decades ago.

Much of what the young child experiences reflects the Inventive metaphoric mode. Yet the differences are simple. The infant does not *have* Formal Operations capability, whereas adults usually do. But what most adults do not have is the child's *attitude to invent* and the strongly affiliating sensory skills that go along with it. Thus there is a tragic tradeoff that certainly Piaget never intended to happen. *The intellect generally matures at the expense of sensorimotor skills.* Reasoning steadily overwhelms sensing. The senses that are most effective in nurturing Formal Operations are enhanced, and the others are herded by rational forces into prisons of propriety where they atrophy into withered ghosts of the forms of knowing they once were.

Nearly two decades ago our schools adopted wholesale the rituals of rationality. This rational focus has nurtured an ecology of what psychologists have labeled the "cognitive" domain. The domain of thought and reason, it is the behavior elicited by the motivational forces of intellect. Emotion, the second great motivator, is the quality assigned to the "affective" domain. It is the arena of feelings, values, and notions of self worth. Good feelings *are* sought after by our schools. But too often they interpret "good" feelings as those you have when you do a rational task accurately. The cherished values are those that lead to the mastery of rational skills and competencies.

104

How about sexuality? This final motivator is usually included in what is called the Psychomotor domain. By my definition, sexuality is involved *any time the human body is used in participational experiences*. This extends the former category, Psychomotor, into a realm which includes genitality but where genitality is not the primary focus, as has been the case in the prevailing use of the word "sexuality." Sexuality as I define it is intimately linked to the Integrative metaphoric mode . . . where the body becomes the medium of exploration. In most instances, the use of one's body in experiential things is relegated to the physical education department within a school. There children are taught to follow the rules of sports. Competitive sports. The surrogate for warfare. *Thus children are tacitly taught that their sexuality is a medium for war.*

The almost paranoic overemphasis on the rational and linear functions of mind is responsible for the rising incidence of gastric ulcers among eight-year-olds who in their third year of school are already being groomed for Stanford and M.I.T. It is also responsible for the "you can't tell the players without a scorecard" syndrome. Whenever human beings say something in an ecology of overextended rationality, they are greeted with "what evidence do you have to back that up?" This attitude discourages taking risks. It diminishes the acknowledgment and celebration of the metaphoric. The rational realms are safe. They stay within the rules. Paradoxical as it seems, the rational mind prefers the rules it invents to the process of invention.

In beauty may I walk. All day long may I walk.
Through the returning seasons may I walk. Beauty I will possess again.
Navajo prayer, Night Way

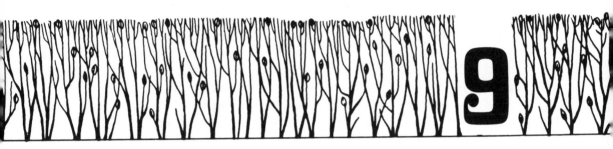

sources of metaphor

The ultimate source of metaphor is nature. Just as nature includes humans, so too does it provide the wellsprings of metaphor. In a long study of incoming students at Harvard psychologists administered a series of imaginative tests of creative potential. Inherent in these tests were indicators of the richness of metaphor. It was found that students from rural backgrounds were far more facile with metaphoric thinking than those from urban centers. The explanation was at once surprising and deceptively simple. Urban environments are at least one generation removed from their natural counterparts. Gordon and others have determined that the richest source of metaphor is nature. Just as nature is infinitely repatternable, its combinations and juxtapositions of elements are incredibly high. Culture-dominated settings are filtered through cultural preferences. In our culture, dominated by a technocratic Judeo-Christian heritage, such phenomena as metamorphosis and transmutation are rare. Both metamorphosis and transmutation refer to processes in which remarkable change is built into the natural

108

scheme — change that results in a phenomenally new kind of being or substance without outside intervention. In cultural systems, intervention must nearly always be deliberate. In nature, such occurrences are commonplace. Accordingly, nature comes up with more options than a setting dominated by cultural alternatives.

The rural students were more used to "down on the farm" relationships with natural cycles. A farmer often knows when to plant, when to irrigate, and when to harvest without consulting a calendar. Those linked to the earth by rural occupations are more alert to natural cycles than those locked in the highly artificial environments of urban life.

Imagine yourself experiencing the following event: It is the first frost of winter. The air temperature and humidity have joined forces to create a furry frost on many objects in your environment. Close your eyes for a moment before you read on and visualize the event first in a rural setting and then in an urban setting. When you've finished, do the same for the first springtime appearance of a green plant in both places. Thoreau writes:

> Every tree, shrub and spire of grass, that could raise its head above the snow, was covered with a dense ice-foliage, answering, as it were, leaf for leaf to its summer dress . . . . It struck me that these ghost leaves, and the green ones whose forms they assume, were the creatures of but one law; that in obedience to the same law the vegetable juices swell gradually into the perfect leaf, on the one hand, and the crystalline particles troop to their standards in the same order on the other..As if the material were indifferent, but the law one and invariable . . . . This foliate structure is common to the coral and the plumage of birds, and to how large a part of animate and inanimate nature . . . . *

Urban students were usually working with second or third generation metaphors. As a result, the reservoir upon which they could draw was already more barren than that available to rural students. What's more, the metaphors that were used by urban students were far less complex than those drawn upon by rural students. Phrases such as, "Slow as . . ." were often finished by rural students as "a pregnant cow with diarrhea," while urban students would finish with ". . . a '49 Ford." I will leave it to the reader to compare the two images to see which is richest in alternatives.

*Thoreau, Henry David. *The Portable Thoreau.* Carl Bode, Editor. Viking Press, New York, 1947.

An urban student, often more facile with language, can generate long lists of metaphors. Upon examining such lists, I have found blandness and sterility compared to the fewer but more generic items on the lists of students closer to natural settings. The "book-smart" students are not metaphorically impoverished by any means. Rather they tend to be rich in metaphoric prowess leading them *away from nature and deeper into the metaphors of cultural consensus*. The rural or nature-close students tend to utilize metaphors that have inherently more generalizability. The natural metaphors celebrate and proliferate alternatives while the cultural metaphors standardize and limit the alternatives.

This all prompted me to write an article first read at a Congressional hearing in 1962 and published professionally three years later defending the preservation of wilderness areas on grounds that few defended at the time. Environmental hearings were replete with those who defended their preservation on recreational and esthetic grounds. But one can only imagine the incredulous looks on the faces of those who heard me argue for wilderness areas to be set aside as reservoirs of metaphor and cathedrals of creativity.

111

More recently such claims are commonplace. Nature is no longer looked upon as mere ornament. It is now being considered primal . . . as a universal womb that all can understand and benefit from to the limits born of their own cultural conditioning. City dwellers in New York state were among the most vociferous and aggressive when Congressmen from Arizona wanted to build dams in the Grand Canyon. Many believed that the Canyon was in Colorado which they thought was next to California. But in spite of their geographic innocence, they defended the natural. Hundreds of thousands of indoor plants are finding their way into urban offices and city apartments. Among the fastest growing businesses in the nation are the suppliers of living plants for homes and industry.

Backyard vegetable gardens and window-box onions and radishes are popping up from coast to coast. True, some who garden give as their motive ready-made rationalizations related to frugality and the cost of living. But deeper reasons appear in the quiet urge to return to more cyclical, more natural processes. Metaphor is born in the natural processes and humans, despite their cultural setting, are first and foremost a product of nature. Humans are natural animals first and cultural citizens second.

Biologists, embryologists, and paleontologists use a phrase that in a sense is one of the more metaphoric statements in science. *Ontogeny recapitulates phylogeny.* The egg develops in a way that is parallel to the way the species has evolved from more primitive forms. Before fertilization the one-celled sperm and ovum are metaphors for all the one-celled life that once populated the ancient seas. Later, as more complex life forms developed, multicellular forms emerged. These creatures are reflected in the embryo by the hollow sac-like bag of cells that forms just prior to the stage in which the stomach and internal organs fold in upon themselves and begin the long journey toward the vertebrate forms. Salamanders, frogs, and fish are all part of this process. Eventually the embryo begins to look uniquely human. But its journey has been a metaphoric tracing of the evolution of species.

Thus in a very real way each human *is* the species. The human is the sum of all the forms of life that have gone before. In a more superficial way the human becomes acculturated in a fashion that parallels phylogenetic development. The steps of intellectual development described by Piaget are perfect metaphors for the way culture emerged to dominate the species. As Alexander Marshack pointed out, culture was born when humans shifted from cyclical or storied time to linear or sequenced time. In a sense, what Marshack described for the species is what Piaget describes for the individual. As children go from the Sensorimotor to the Formal Operations stage in intellectual development, they effectively trace the pattern of evolution of Western culture from the cyclic-ordered world of Neanderthal humans to the linear-ordered, culture-dominated world of modern *Homo sapiens*.

Humans have lived the metaphors of both their biological *and* their cultural heritage. However, like the last person we have loved, the most recent — the cultural heritage — is the freshest in our memory. Thus I propose the most tentative of speculations on the origins of metaphor. As we encounter culture, we raise the ghosts of only the last ten to twenty thousand years of human existence. As we encounter nature we raise the winds of five billion years of natural existence. There is *more* of nature.

113

One of the more popular, culturally approved ways of returning to nature is the growing trend toward natural childbirth. Men and women spend several weeks in classes that deal with the phenomenon of birth. Together they learn that birth is not akin to having a gall bladder removed or amputating a limb. Rather, the partners are deculturalized. They are stripped of the second- and third-generation cultural prejudices about birth. They learn the rhythmic sequences implanted by nature in the genetic stuff of humans. They learn that it is work, it is joy, and, like most natural things, it is a bit messy.

The male is prepared for the pain and for the control, once natural but now acculturated out, that can be willfully exerted . . . and for the joy of those moments. The man must be ready to re-enter culture, however. He will not be "one of the boys" when he returns to work. Of his acquaintances, only one of twenty knows the experience of the delivery room. Most are experts about the couches, the cigarettes, and the dog-eared magazines in the waiting room. Few can speak of the tension in their partner's face as the cyclic-time contractions bunched together and were measured on the delivery room clock in linear time. Most will know nothing of contractions but will speak in the linearities of minutes and hours instead. Their only acknowledgement of cyclic time might be in numbers of cigarettes smoked! The delivery room is far richer in sources of metaphor than the waiting room. Both have metaphors, but one is closer to nature than the other.

Nature is as accessible as a mountain, a delivery room, or a diet. One's body is natural. Movement, jogging, and the martial arts are all reservoirs of new levels of natural awareness. All are sources of richer metaphors. George Leonard, futurist, educator, and author of the seminal book of the seventies, *The Transformation,* is a resounding spokesperson for the body as a total sense organ. His interest in the martial art of aikido is a joy to behold. Once, when discussing it, his eyes drifted into that kind of look that goes both inward and outward. He said, "It's like momentarily getting hooked into the universe . . . for a moment you begin to move like the planets move."

I know after watching little children for years that there is far more to learning than the simple act of being able to operate more fully in abstractions such as reading, writing, and arithmetic. Children in the first eighteen months of life in what Piaget calls the Sensorimotor stage are thought by many developmental scientists to be gaining refinement of muscle control as they crawl, creep, and generally wiggle about in their environment. I see this as a limited conclusion. Brain researchers have long ago pointed out that with electrode stimulation of various areas of the brain, the "knowing" that is stored there is retrieved. But much to everyone's surprise, the *emotion* or feeling that was stored with that knowing comes *first*. This probably means that everything we know is coded into the neuronal network in our brains in at least two ways — culturally approved or rational knowing and natural or metaphoric knowing. In other words, all that we "know" is stored in both metaphor and logic.

The incredible chauvinism of adultism has a tendency to ignore anything that is not encoded in the specific, straightforward logic of language or logical reasoning. Children who explore the world using senses we have now forgotten often do so through their mouths. Oh yes, the Freudians would say, "an oral fixation," "obviously looking for a breast substitute." These same logical minds once said that children could not smile until they were at least two months old. These same logical thinkers justified the tendency to slap and quickly sever a newborn infant's umbilicus to get it to start breathing! After all, babies weren't people yet.

And then came Frederick Leboyer. That gentle maverick of a French physician who began caring as much for the soulfeeding of the child as for the mother. And certainly more for both mother and child than for the precious schedule of the delivery-room clinicians. The little girl born at the beginning of this book would have had a marvelously different delivery had she entered the world by Leboyer's method. First, she would enter without bright lights and scurry. She might feel the second human ever to touch her placing fingers under her arms to invite her through the vaginal opening. She would be held with a deep, abiding gentleness that communicates profound respect for her as a human.

The hands would begin a deep, thorough massage of her with umbilicus still attached. She would be placed in the hollow "nest" of her mother's now-empty abdomen. There she would again feel the warmth she had known all her first nine months of life. She would feel the touching and caressing born of love, and her first moments of "learning" of the world into which she was born would involve her entire body. The ultimate sense organ. She has not "learned" yet to specialize the modes through which she gains access to experience. Much later she will be trained to forget all the routes she now has and will be encouraged to submit to the idea that there are "five" senses. Her access to the universe will be culturally limited to five holes in a sphere of perception. And she will learn and grow in ways that will constrict the dozens of perceptions given by nature into the narrow channel consistent with the cultural view of human capacities.

But in Leboyer's approach her tiny body is still a sensory cathedral. *After* she has started breathing of her own volition . . . without the ritual slapping or joustling . . . *then* the umbilicus is severed. As long as it is intact the child need not breathe. She still gets her oxygen from her mother. But once she becomes a "creature of the air," the umbilicus can be cut. She is gently taken from her mother and immersed in a water bath that again surrounds her with the feel of a world known well for nine full months. She moves, reaches, and *begins to play!* "No!" the guardians of the cultural order would shout. To say the child is at play would be folly! But nonetheless she plays! And then, as if wonders would

117

never cease, the child smiles! This, the most joyful affront of all to the staid theorists who demand that birth be a terrifying, anguished experience. Within twenty-four hours, many infants born this way smile and frequently some even issue forth deep-throated laughter.

All this leads me to the holistic conclusion that whenever any "learning" is taking place, *all* the sensory capacities operate at once. Thus those things narrowly called knowledge become encoded at once in our central nervous system as well as in our brains. Along with "learning" in the intellectual sense are all those other qualities of knowing belonging to the forgotten and culturally discredited ways of sensing. The emotionality and sexuality that accompany experience *too* are encoded in the central nervous system and the brain. This is not to suggest that the nerve network has a memory of content, but rather one of process and of sensation. Some might say the total gestalt of the moment of learning is preserved in knowing.

Just as the image of a dripping lemon causes the tongue to move and tense up and the jaw muscles to tighten almost reflexively, the opposite is true. Tensing the tongue and the jaw muscles elicits the image of the lemon. But even more than just the lemon. It may call to mind

a pitcher frosty with gaudy pink flowers on the outside. It was the kind that you're given for getting a ten gallon fillup from an attendant that looks too hot and has grease on his white suit. I've always wondered why the gas station folks have white suits . . . . There is dew on the outside of the pitcher and you and your brother got to cut the lemons because you were big enough now and you remembered that you had to clean off the knife because you were told that the lemon juice would make the steel all dark and brown. Later you and your brother dared each other to eat all the leftover stuff from inside a half lemon until it made a clean white cup. Oh the taste! It made your tongue curl up and your jaws get all tense. You also remember how frightened you got because you wondered if old people whose teeth were brown got that way from eating lemons . . . . (response in guided imagery workshop)

Acupuncture has demonstrated that the stimulation of various nerve centers outside the brain results in a whole host of images and contexts being rejuvenated in the mind. Little research has yet been aimed at linking these to cause-effect qualities of the simultaneous acquisition I spoke of. George Leonard, mentioned earlier, has been the most articulate spokesperson about how body and mind are transformed by celebrating movement, exercise, and use. His book *The Ultimate Athlete* goes deeply into the qualities of returning to more complete awarenesses of one's physicalness to pursue transformation of psychic being. His work is an anthem to the function and philosophy of the Integrative and Inventive modes of metaphoric knowing.

That the totality of knowing is locked into physical acts is well known to those who provide therapy to victims of rape. The very act of returning to genital sexuality with a chosen partner often elicits the intellectual, emotional, and sexual knowing that were encoded during the brutality of rape.

A woman whom I once counseled in metaphoric thought had been raped just prior to our work together. Each night since the assault she had recurring dreams of the horror. I asked her to lie back, close her eyes, and relive the dream. As she did, her whole body reacted. Her muscles twitched spasmodically and hardened; her eyes darted about beneath her lids like exaggerated REM sleep; her hands became clammy and cold and eventually her stomach convulsed and she sat up terrified. Her entire body remembered. We were able to get an equilibrium through night dreaming within a few days by having her struggle to stay asleep during the dream. Once she did so her body still "remembered," but it also knew she could control the effect of the knowing. She could survive the experience, just as she had in "real life." The dream never returned.

119

Once when I was working in a creativity workshop in Iowa, an older woman wanted desperately to write poetry about her youth in rural corn country. I asked her what she used to do that she would like to write about. Among her answers was "husking corn." I told her to wait and I dashed out and bought a half dozen ears of corn in a supermarket. When I returned I had her sit as she used to and encouraged her to visualize the setting. With her eyes closed, and sitting as she remembered, I had her husk corn. In less than ten minutes she produced her first poem. Within an hour, she had written nearly a dozen. Now I hear she has published some of them. She simply asked her body to harvest what experience had sown. In effect the metaphors of the natural experience were locked within her. She chose to use sexuality (using her body as a sense organ) to recreate access to the knowing.

The total human is part of the natural world. The fragmented human is part of the cultural equation. Using the full spectrum of metaphoric-mode experience resurrects the "naturalness" of previous experience. The rational or linear modes fragment the original experience and specify the access routes. In effect the rational or linear mind limits the experience as well as the access to it. Metaphor transforms the limits of experience and the limits of knowing into the more synergic and holistic qualities of the natural systems.

121

To summarize, then . . . the richest source of metaphor is nature. Ultimately humans are natural beings, though of late, say the last 20,000 years, humans have systematically surrendered that naturalness by erecting a cultural filter between themselves and the natural world. The greatest reservoir of metaphor comes from ultimate sources . . . the natural. *A secondary source of metaphor comes from culture.*

For example, it is highly unlikely that early humans invented housing without first having looked at beehives, barnacle clusters, or bird nests. So few of the primates other than humans build houses or shelters that we might well presume the practice came from need *and* cerebral competence. To study a beehive one must also study bees. Their habits, food-getting, storage, social rituals, and hive-making are all part of the experience. But archaeologists, when studying the ruins of ancient cultures, seldom think of bees. Instead they superimpose their own modern cultural context regarding dwellings upon the earlier culture. What this does in effect is to compound abstractions. The early humans abstracted from nature. Those who followed most likely abstracted from the dwellings of the first culture. Two or three hundred generations later, modern humans are working with incredibly abstracted abstractions . . . unless they too, return to the original sources of nature.

Perhaps in the contexts of Freud, the greatest source of metaphor would be the primary processes; the poorest would be the secondary processes. Some researchers such as Ornstein have accepted the presence of hemispheric differentiation models that could, with little effort, be considered cathedrals of primary and secondary processes. Or in our more current terminology, the left cerebral hemisphere houses ordering of linear time, secondary access to cultural metaphors, and the filters that screen, organize, and systematize experience into "reality." The right cerebral hemisphere contains processing of cyclical time, primary access to natural metaphors, and the freedom to reinstate all of the twenty or more natural senses in the presence of the natural reality.

The sources of metaphor are everywhere, but continued acquisition of culturally filtered resources is metaphorically linked to eating a diet of foods that are 100% manufactured for you in germ-free kitchens and packaged in human made containers. It is not that culturally filtered metaphors are right or wrong! It is simply that they represent the product of a kind of cultural censorship that is not protected by the first amendment to the Constitution. Their effect is tacit, not direct. Subtle, not violent.

Natural sources of metaphor defy being censored. Because there is no censor save the human that perceives them, each of *us* becomes the filter for natural metaphors if we accept the cultural premise. Thus we must each accept responsibility for the system with which our allegience lies . . . nature or culture.

Museums and zoos with embalmed or imprisoned abbreviations of nature are cherished cultural institutions. Art, a symbolic visual metaphor, is also cherished by cultures. There is safety for cultures that transform nature into cultural statements. Galleries, museums, and the exorbitant cultural energy medium of money are all invested in the process of sanctifying the derivative at the expense of the natural. The person who attacked Michelangelo's *Pieta* seems far more horrible to the culture than the people who bulldoze mountains away to build housing. My comments certainly should not be construed to denigrate art, but rather to exaggerate the double standard that exists. Nevertheless a new attitude is clearly emerging. Many specifically culture-based movements are literally losing ground to the preservation of natural settings. This attitude is in vital opposition to the artifice of nature caught under glass and confined behind bars.

Anyone who tells me that my emotions or desires don't exist is in effect telling me that *I* don't exist.

—Abraham Maslow

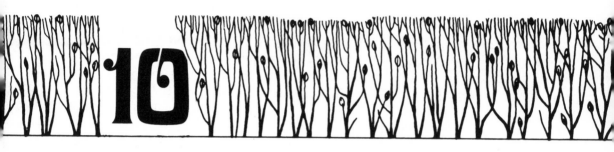

motivation and metaphor

Stimulation is the lifeblood of action in cultural systems. Motivation in turn is the lifeblood of action in natural systems. The difference? Stimulation is extrinsic. It is external. It starts *outside* whoever is getting stimulated. Motivation is intrinsic. It is born *inside* the organism calling itself into action. This means that *I can stimulate you but only YOU can motivate you.* Without exception, cultural institutions have been set up throughout history to control and limit the actions of the members of that culture. That is, the things that sociologists and anthropologists call cultural mores are in fact checklists of the kinds of things it is appropriate to be motivated toward. And these are agreed upon by the culture. They become lists of cultural "do's and don't's."

What the culture does after coming to agreement about the "rules," is to set up a cultural ecology that provides constant stimulation. This is to ensure that the cultural members will "play the game." Many scientists have studied the differences in mores and cultural rules and have assumed that once mores are created, they become the force that guides the motivation of the culture. That's a complicated way of saying that many assume the rules of the game are more important than the players.

125

The mores or guiding values of a culture appear in subtle as well as obvious ways. Our coins and paper currency are themselves a cultural stimulator in that they are artificial cultural substitutes for natural goods. A dime becomes an apple or two carrots or perhaps a turnip and a half. A piece of highly specialized paper becomes ten dimes and can purchase some bread and a quart of milk. Imagine the routine that a comedian could develop showing Stuyvesant trying to convince the Native Americans that these cultural metaphors were in fact as valuable as large parcels of natural landscape.

Beyond that is the tacit reminder of another external: "In God we trust" is emblazoned on each piece of our money. Flags, churches, and, in a more commercial sense, trademarks and other visual or abstract symbolic images are hung about with the hope of stimulating us to get involved at one level or another. Jonas Salk once characterized culture as a metabiological secretion. From one perspective this is true. For so very few of the cultural artifacts are really linked to the satisfaction of "basic" human needs, food, shelter, and reproduction. Most of what culture has produced serves as an anthem to the institutions of society. And the institutions are the filing cabinets of the rules.

But cultures have to keep their own games going. There has to be a way to enforce the rules. The way most cultures have chosen is the way that psychologist B.F. Skinner teaches pigeons to play ping pong . . . by external stimulation. By providing a reward when a particular response is demonstrated, humans and pigeons can be conditioned to do a wide variety of things. Cultures stimulate (or provide rewards) by setting up the institutions as the only game in town. When there is only one game in town, it is easy to tell who is playing and who is watching (and who is winning). In such settings humans who don't play often are made to feel guilty. Those who do play are made to feel rewarded. Under the ever-present pressure, most nonplayers join in. The psychological result is a kind of unacknowledged confusion. Members of a culture are always exposed to the stimulation of being held to "belong." Yet if they think they do not want to (are motivated to do something else), they are made to feel the pressure to join in. Cultures thrive on creating a kind of confusion between motivation and stimulation.

For those who wish to control, this confusion is a Machiavellian gift. The rules or mores of a culture are usually couched in religion or law, two of the most formalized and rational qualities of culture. Most cultures ritualize both law and religion. The result is that if any confusion reigns in the minds of individuals in the culture, the rituals and the experiences individuals have as they participate in the rituals are usually strong enough to foster the idea that the culture is real and that nature is not.

For example, if I do not know that I can control my own motivational tendencies, then I will be easy prey for those who want to engage me in their ritualistic stimulation. Upon experiencing one of these cultural rituals — a baptism, marriage, funeral or even the senior prom — I may be thrilled, awed, frightened, overjoyed, or any of a number of other emotional reactions by the power with which my culture communicates to me its mores. I will be hyperstimulated. I will be emotionally imprinted. My heart will pound; tears may form; I may feel the swell of pride and awe at the might of my culture. And then I will be reinforced by being told that this is right, that it is good, and that it carries honor.

Brain-stimulation studies have shown that factual information is linked in the brain's storage networks with the emotion that was present when the information was acquired. This means that what I *felt* when I learned something was stored along with what I *learned*. What better way for a culture to maintain control over the metaphoric mind than to ritualize the schemes in which learning takes place? The more varied and emotionally vivid the ritual, the more rapidly and completely will the individual substitute the qualities of stimulation for motivation. In other words, one of the things cultural rituals do is to create highly charged emotional settings to imprint a particular kind of knowing. Examples of these might be the ritual singing of the national anthem at sports events or the swearing of an oath of honesty on a Bible in a courtroom. Through history, cultures have used emotionally charged rituals to create attitudes of blind conformity to the rules or values of that culture. Adolph Hitler was perhaps the most recent genius in this arena.

The individual in such a ritual-laden culture is subject to confusion between motivation and stimulation. Because the culture makes those who walk its fringes feel insecure and somewhat unsure of their role, they are ripe for conversion. This insecurity in a ritualized atmosphere of mild deprivation creates an environment in which humans are particularly susceptible to persuasion. In the politest terms it is an emotionally stimulating experience designed to fulfill. In crudest terms it is brainwashing. Cultists of all sorts have used such strategies, and their most willing subjects are those who have generally responded to stimulation to guide their lives. When they did experiment with motivation, they felt guilty. Socially induced or presumed guilt is the meadowland of psychological predators.

It becomes almost impossible to separate individuals' responses to cultural stimulation from intrinsic motivation. What happens is that individuals internalize willingly (or by force) the ritual stimuli of their culture. Upon questioning members of cultures, researchers find that they do not know the differences between the stimulation created by the ritual and their own motivation. And judging by most of the published data in social psychology, sociology, and anthropology, neither do the researchers.

129

Edward Hall, for example, reports the results of a talented Anglo filmmaker's attempts at understanding movies made by Navajo people. The filmmaker criticized the structure, form, and sequencing of the Native American cinematographers. Hall, with the compassionate acceptance born of years of being near the Navajo, asked the filmmaker to reverse his procedure and use his critique of the Navajo techniques as a statement of his own techniques. That is, he turned the criticism of the Navajo film techniques into a mirror image of his own culture. He saw that what he perceived to be lacking in Navajo film work was in fact a statement of our culture's prejudices in regard to what constitutes "good film." This experience resulted in a vividly enlightening portrait of Anglo cultural bias in the "science" of filmmaking.

It has recently been reported that Piaget is trying to research the parallelism between the historical (cultural) evolution of Western humankind and his own developmental stages. I presumed this linkage some years ago when I studied Piaget as a cultural spokesperson rather than a psychologist. As I did so, it was obvious to me that his bias toward Western intellectual dominance was a product of his acculturization. Thus it strikes me as circular that he is now interested in proving this relationship.

Many scholars of culture simply do not know the difference between motivation and stimulation. They focus on the behavior of a culture and presume all behavior observed is linked directly to the individual motivation of that cultural member. Even empirical psychology seems confused, judging by the nature of the research pouring forth. So confused are the "scientific psychologists" that they define psychology as the science of behavior. It is through the medium of behavior that psychologists and other social scientists speculate about motivation. The majority of research contains precious little information about human motivation that isn't baldly confused with cultural stimulation. It is more confusing the deeper one delves. Since intrinsic motivation is so elusive, many social theorists label culturally approved of qualities of motivation as *innate*. Plainly this is the easiest way out.

I recently worked with young black adults in Harlem. They had been identified by specialists as reading at the third and fourth grade level although they were in high school. On one occasion this same group were convulsed with laughter as they read the jokes printed on the final page of a *Playboy* centerfold. Not only were the jokes at an adult reading level, but they were written for the dominant cultural context. When I asked the students about this apparent discrepancy in their reading abilities, they weren't "can't readers." They were "won't readers." Meaning that they *chose* not to read. I later found out that this was interpreted by them as their only way to "get the man." That is, it was their only way to strike back at a system that they felt persecuted them. The system, on the other hand, perceived them as losers and in-competents and genetically deficient at worst, at best as "culturally deprived."

The dominant culture's assumption was that competence equaled language facility — and facility in the standard dialect, at that. The minority-culture values were related to resisting the power of a dominant force. Further probing revealed that the students were *not* anti-reading . . . they were *pro-human*. They felt reading and language skills had been systematically used to destroy the real talents they had. They were street-smart, what I would call Ph.D. level street-smart, but they were in a system which judged people as competent *only* on the criteria of book-smart.

How this works is quite obvious if one thinks cyclically, but it makes no sense in linear thought. If I can't see inside your motives, I look instead to what I can see . . . your behavior. Of course, once I see and record your behavior I still can't see inside your motives. *But I can pretend I can.* I look to those things I can see outside you, and they are clustered around you like ornaments on a Christmas tree. They are the institutions and artifacts. Since I can see them, I presume they do in fact *motivate* you. If I am sensitive to the original definition of motivation, I must accommodate by saying "extrinsic" motivation! This is a clearcut substitute for the word *stimulation.*

The cyclic part is yet to come. Remember that I cannot see your motivation, but I can see your behavior. I see the cultural stimuli and so I link *them* to your behavior. And here's where the cycle gets completed. I substitute qualities of cultural stimulation for motivation, and then I judge motivation, behavior, and cultural mores as if they were tightly dependent upon each other. As I said earlier, this argument does not hold up in linear thought but it becomes obvious in cyclic reasoning. The strange part is that it has survived so long in the presence of empirical scientific philosophy so vividly linear and so vocally abusive to circular arguments.

Those whose philosophy is aimed at controlling the individual are those who must either control or deny the existence of motivation. They must convince the individual that their human reward, their virtue and honor, is linked to conforming to cultural stimulation. The most effective strategy for such "controllers" is to emphasize and enforce stimulation as a substitute for motivation. They praise conformity and are terrified of will in people. When humans discover, as so many are doing now, that they do in fact have significant control over their own will and thus their own motivation, the sense of personal freedom that emerges transcends all of the cultural ornamentation.

Of all of those who fear human will and the concept of intrinsic motivation, none is more articulate than Burrhus Frederick Skinner of Harvard. In his classic studies of behavior, Skinner clearly documents the compulsion to create a philosophy of control. Moving out of behavioral research laboratories after more than two decades of study, Skinner in *Beyond Freedom and Dignity* offered a social version of the controllers' society. He calls for a forceful application of scientific logic to be brought to bear to form the cultural mores and stimulation patterns toward which the society can be conditioned. He calls for techniques, strategies, and institutions to develop a more forceful role in setting up the stimulus environments to mold the behavior of the citizens.

Behavior modification is the primary strategy of the stimulus-response mentality. It uses various schemes of reward and punishment to stimulate humans into particular patterns of behavior. In behavior modification strategies, the controllers try to convince the subjects that they should be "motivated" to conform to the chosen behavior patterns. In schools and prisons where behavior modification is used, the most startling results are achieved with humans who deviate most from norms. That is, it works best with the most mentally, emotionally, and physically abnormal. Substituting stimulation and conditioning for motivation is easiest with social, psychological, and physical deviates.

When one uses behavior modification with "normal" subjects, one quickly finds that it does not work the same way. In fact it may well be counterproductive. Recent studies have shown that *positive reinforcement*, a strategy of behavior modification using compliments and praise as rewards for specific behavior, tends to destroy the subjects' long-term interest. Students with whom positive reinforcement has been used often "improve" their performance at first. This improvement encourages the researchers to claim great value for their method. But soon the students begin to sense coercion and deception. They begin to feel cheated and tricked. This negative emotion becomes linked with the material that they were studying. Later when the reinforcement is removed or the students receiving it realize they can choose whether or not to continue, the choice is most often to quit. It is almost as though the mind, bombarded by behavior-modification strategies, eventually gets the chance to rest and reflect — and opts out. Even the rational mind, the conforming mind, cannot accept deceit in those experiences that ordinarily nourish it.

Where is the metaphoric mind in all of this? Most simply stated . . . the metaphoric mind is the adversary of cultural conformity. The metaphoric mind "feeds" on stimuli . . . it digests them and transforms them into substance for motivation. The metaphoric mind is a reservoir of motivation. If cultural suppression of the individual is to succeed, then suppression of the metaphoric mind and of motivation must take place. Religions and laws are the most common forms of cultural consensus statements. But beyond simply creating law and religion, the culture must enforce the way these institutions perform motivational and metaphoric suppression. The institutions that formalize this suppression are myriad; they are schools, courts, churches, sports, the media, etc. However, the most pervasive quality of suppression of motivation and metaphor is the near total acceptance of the very philosophy of linearity and mental conformity called rationality.

Far more than any specific cultural institution, the philosophy of rational, linear logic permeates *all* the corners of our social system. Tacit emphasis on consensus, agreement, and convergence of purpose creates a cultural milieu that favors the rational mind and fears the metaphoric mind. Thus cultural forces tacitly reward behavioral responses to stimulation more than behavioral responses to intrinsic motivation. Unless of course the person has the (highly unlikely) intrinsic motivation to conform. The person who has achieved perfection in the controlling society is a person whose only intrinsic motivation is to emulate B.F. Skinner's pigeons and rats and do the bidding of the controller at every turn.

What then, is the difference between the willess stimulation-seeker who has given up motivational control and the highly intrinsic, motivated person?

The difference is a function of how fully and comfortably the person acknowledges and celebrates the metaphoric mind. But even more important is how fully the person integrates the use of the metaphoric mind with the rational mind. The results of such integration have in my experience produced humans who demonstrate the degree of high ego strength that goes with what is commonly called . . . mental health.

What this means is that child, homemaker, executive, farmer, and long-living person all have high ego strength and good mental health if

135

they possess the courage, humor, and flexibility of equilibrium between their minds.

Educational level does not seem to matter. A higher level of formal education is beneficial primarily to the left, rational hemisphere. Thus many people with low levels of formal education may still reach a measure of equilibrium between rational and metaphoric modes. My suspicion is that most neurosis is a product of disequilibrium between the mind-modes. This would include both rational and nonrational neuroses . . . but more about that later.

Investigators in personality theory have often studied the human ego. Unfortunately the result has been a bewildering muddle of currents and countercurrents representing the overall theoretical picture. In recent decades a host of psychologists and psychiatrists have tried to unravel the Gordian knot tied by Freud and his translators. Few have done much to simplify the issues, but one particularly insightful researcher seems to have come up with the basis of a workable model of personality. That psychologist is O.J. Harvey at the University of Colorado, and his work led to the formulation of "core" personalities. I have modified his work so as to be able to exploit its metaphoric nature as well as its rational basis. Harvey felt that many researchers and theorists were too confused by the trees to deal with the forest. So in a manner akin to an ecologist, he searched for the overall picture of what was happening in the context of personality in one small but vitally significant slice of human endeavor. He studied meaning and consistency of behavior and its relationship to motivation in stress conditions.

When people are "cool" and not under stress, they show such a bewildering array of behaviors that no one knows for certain what it all means. Harvey wanted to study that clearcut, pure condition that emerged when motivation and behavior were directly linked. So he looked for people under stress. Once he found them it became obvious that there were far greater consistencies in their behavior when stress was present than when things were flowing easy and comfortable. Hundreds if not thousands of these observations resulted in his establishing categories of behavior-motivation linkage that took the form of what I call "core" personalities.

In each of these categories, people tended to respond with remarkable consistency when stress occurred. Further, it became obvious that it was a hazard to generalize about stress itself. One person's stress was another's picnic. The thing that could be generalized about was that the behavior of each of the types could be predicted reliably when the stress appeared. The "core" types (which I have modified slightly from Harvey's work) I have called Authoritarian, Dependency, and Intrinsic. I have gone into these in some greater detail elsewhere, so I will describe them briefly here.* What I want to emphasize here is not the details of these types, but the relationship between the types and the disequilibrium between the rational and metaphoric minds.

*Samples, Bob, and Bob Wohlford. *Opening: A primer for Self-Actualization.* Addison-Wesley Publ. Co., Reading, Mass., 1973.

The Authoritarian Core is the "true believer." This person's allegiance is to a message or faith that is in his or her view irrefutably true. The content of the message doesn't matter to Authoritarians. It is more important that they feel they know the truth. To cover their tracks, Authoritarians build great rational towers of interrelated, intermeshed "facts." And each fact is presumed true and real. When challenged, they look past you with the gaze of the divinely inspired. They tend to argue only to a point. When that point is reached, then whoever disagrees with them is banished to some version of hell as a lost soul worthy of no more energy. It doesn't matter whether Authoritarians preach about physics, politics, art, or macrobiotic food: they brook no compromise. Their tactic is to divide and conquer. But they do so for the "lord" . . . and the "lord" may be Isaac Newton, Carl Rogers, Karl Marx, or Kate Millett. These people are almost always rational zealots in their thought mode.

The Dependency Core will fly under any flag or movement or posture one can imagine. Dependency people are abysmal when alone and depend on others to fulfill their manipulative needs. Their role is to subvert, convert, win over, and control. Where Authoritarians take you into their fold or kill you (ignore you), the Dependency person can never ignore you. The Dependency person may control you or invest in being controlled *by* you. Either way you must exist or their life equation adds up to zero. They have in both their rational and metaphoric mind-modes a great scorecard of what they have done for you and what you have done *to* them. They may well use the guise of rationality, metaphor, lies, or tears, but their motivation is always focused on manipulating themselves into a better position *with* you — or a better position *than* you. They may be positive or negative, but they are always compelled to control others. Nearly all of this control is motivated by their presumption of emotional, intellectual, or sexual deficiencies in themselves or others. They tend to need others to provide the *stimulational vacuum* into which they delight in being drawn.

139

Before introducing the third type, let us reflect momentarily upon these first two. Both are deeply committed to extrinsic stimulation. Authoritarians are causebound to things outside themselves. Their missionary zeal is a manifestation of total immersion in some external quality, usually culturally affiliated, and of their compulsion to represent that involvement to the world. They quickly become labeled as zealots or neurotics. Consider, for example, nature lovers who embrace a mission to save every blade of grass in the world. They will often presume a god-given revelation as they busily track down villains to overwhelm. They are true authoritarians and they love to discover infidels as they sanctify the cause. Dependency nature lovers will often join the cause to suffer, to *be* controlled rather than to win. They are themselves with the proper repertoire of symbols (Sierra Club membership, lumberjack jackets, often a beard or the no-washed, no-brushed look). So armed, they seek out others to suffer in the presence of or to make suffer in their presence. But like the Authoritarian, they are responding to extrinsic stimulation, and the motivated behavior is focused on exploiting others for self (or cause) or exploiting self for others (or cause).

This last point is crucial to an understanding of motivation. Our Western heritage, replete with its muddle of dichotomies and dialectic arguments, has forced upon us the opposite meanings of the words "selfish" and "selfless." Selfish is bad in any of our cultural books . . . even capitalism says it's bad. Selfless is good because it justifies externalizing the legitimacy for personal being. (Remember that's what culture wants of individuals.) I argue that both are exploitative postures. To repeat, selfish is an exploitation of others for self. Selfless is an exploitation of self for others. Both are extrinsic.

So let us explore an alternative condition between these two extremes. *Selfness.* When selfness prevails, the qualities of others are sometimes used for self and the qualities of self are often extended to others. *The basic and key difference is that exploitation is never the object or the outcome.*

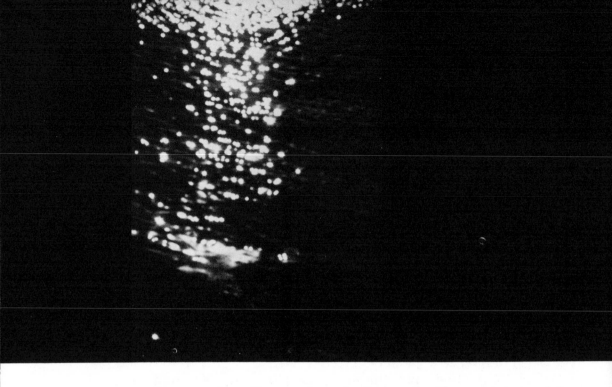

Now to the next Core Personality, the Intrinsic. Characteristic of the Intrinsic core personality type is a completely internalized acceptance of one's responsibility. This means that no extrinsic qualities are sought out when things go awry. Instead, these people go inside themselves to check out the sources of anxiety, either positive or negative. It is true that Intrinsic people sometimes believe strongly in "causes" or issues, and they often enlist others in love or politically focused efforts, *but they always accept the responsibility for their actions*. In the Intrinsic person there is *always* remarkable consistency in the linkage between behavior and motivation. There is high ego strength in this core personality.

The Intrinsic core personality and those that lie beyond it are characterized by such a comfort in the equilibrium between their capacities, actions, and potential that they tend to feel very little stress. When they do they know it is stress *they* create. The Intrinsic people know full well that they are responsibile for their own value-prejudices and are responsible for what they *allow* to disturb them. Intrinsic people tend to get "relaxedly alert" when events that ordinarily cause stress occur. Like good athletes, their body and mind relax and wait for the situation to demand action. In the same way that blood vessels often

dilate and become far more efficient, the mind relaxes and allows the solution to appear.

In the Intrinsic core, behavior and motivation are almost always linked honestly together. Intrinsic people seldom play games but if they do, they admit it freely if in fact they don't announce it at the outset. Children often come up to parents and announce that they are going to pretend they are dragons. It is almost as if they didn't trust others to know it was a game. The Intrinsic core contrasts with Authoritarian and Dependency cores in that the latter have behavior and motivation linked primarily during times of stress. The Intrinsic person experiences very little stress but high behavior-motivation linkage.

The Intrinsic person also has high ego strength. High ego strength almost automatically results when people accept the responsibility for their own actions. When this sense of responsibility is acted on, motivational-behavior equivalency, high ego strength, and high equilibrium between sexuality, emotionality, and intellectuality come together. This in the fullest sense is what I believe Abraham Maslow meant by the term "self-actualization."

Now to theorize a bit further. Recent studies show that relative equilibrium exists between the hemispheres of the brain in creative people. Further, in such people the rational and metaphoric minds seem to be integrated and to achieve high levels of activity together. I believe that the qualities demonstrated by the Intrinsic core personality are the qualities of acceptance of both cerebral hemispheres and the synergic integration of the two.

In contemporary society, this takes high ego strength because of the social tendency toward separation of the mind functions and the denigration of the metaphoric mind. However, long ago when I faced the question about how more vividly healthy creative minds could be nurtured, I sought out not what *inhibited* creativity but what *nurtured* it. As a result, my bias has long been toward what worked, not what failed. I inadvertently followed the lead that Maslow so often and so eloquently championed. He claimed to be interested in the attic of human experience and not the basement.

143

I explored for nearly a decade and a half the kinds of human ecologies that would nurture integration of the minds. I sought the kinds of mini-ecologies that would be so much more exciting and inclusive than the exclusive rationally dominant mega-ecology of contemporary culture. What I found was simple:

Allow humans to be themselves and celebrate that selfness.
Love the metaphoric mind and respect the rational.
Nurture motivation.
Consider any attempt at communication appropriate.
Celebrate the whole person.

In other words, the "goodness" that Maslow saw in humans is really there. But the culture tends to cast itself in the role of censor of the total human. Thus so many with the potential to actualize have constantly been eroded by the stifling control of extrinsic qualities. All my colleagues and I have tried to do is to relinquish stimulation and nurture motivation. To bring each person to an awareness and acceptance of the Intrinsic, the ultimate in manipulation had to occur. We had to tell the people with whom we worked that they were able to manipulate and control themselves. One can hardly imagine people's anguish when we provided them with such input — people who have responded faithfully to the extrinsic all their lives. All the game plans were lost, along with all the crutches and scapegoats. They confronted the terrible knowing that they owned their universe. They created their own joy, their own suffering — and we were unnecessary. We simply had to get out of their way while they affirmed their ownership. The length of time it took varied . . . but it always resulted in an awareness of growth, a feeling of personal vulnerability, and a sense of courage. Motivation is different from stimulation. It's more human . . . more natural.

144

I found out the truth could be said in whatever metaphor we need to communicate with one another.

—Ram Dass

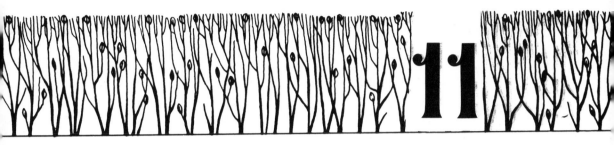

11

the human triangle

As long as humans have looked at themselves in the mirror of experience, they have seen an enigma. History is full of violence and destruction. Seldom have humans enjoyed a time when large numbers could openly express the magic and fulfillment of being human. Why?

To me the answer is clear. Humans have created cultures that systematically deny the fulfillment of the individual. Cultures were born, matured, and died in an awesome parade of variations on the human theme . . . and no culture has systematically nurtured *all* of the qualities of human potential. There has always lurked in the background a social censor . . . one that said *this* is good and *that* is bad. And always those choices have limited the human condition.

Yet in all the experiences I have gained in nurturing motivational actualization, I have been struck by the human goodness. True, there have been tests of whether or not it was real, but basically humans have been so enlivened by allowing themselves to express motivational behavior rather than stimulated behavior that they have slipped quickly from analytical skepticism into expressive, nonexploitative joy.

146

For example: Working with a black teenager named Lionel who had been "led down the road" by an equal dose of tyrants and "lily white liberals," I was struck by the way each of our encounters started from ground zero. Day after day I was being tested anew. I was repeatedly challenged to cease using stimulation and share in expressing my own motivation. Several of my co-workers often asked me, "Why do you go through that shit over and over again?" And my response had to be, "Because somehow I haven't *really* relinquished my role . . . and that kid knows it!"

On one occasion Lionel took an assignment I gave and carried it out "his" way. The assignment was "Go outside and find a million of something and prove it." He left with an "Oh . . . yeeeaah" smile on his face. I felt myself tense and then relax. The relaxation came when I admitted that I was acting like a stimulator whose patterns had gone wrong — a "right stimulus, wrong response" kind of problem. I busied myself with other class members and the teacher as time ticked by.

Then about ten minutes before the class ended, Lionel came back in with an adding machine tape. He looked a bit puzzled and said, "I didn't make it." I asked what it was he hadn't made and found out that the tape was from the office adding machine and bore a list of numbers that came off a piece of paper that was jammed into Lionel's pocket. He showed me the tape and it totalled 875,079. Later Lionel told me that the numbers and the tape represented the mileage taken from the odometers of the cars in the faculty parking lot. In the time he was outside, Lionel had gone into about twenty cars and read the odometers. *And the cars were all locked!*

Even more impressive, in its own way, than that, Lionel had gone to the office and convinced the staff to let him use the adding machine. The office was a place Lionel had religiously avoided in times past. As we talked about all this, it was obvious that Lionel was a person of real courage. He was confident and bright, but few in the dominant culture had enough patience to check this out. By now I was convinced that Lionel was reaching a point where he no longer needed to test me. As a result I was able to see his actions as indicators of courage instead of the bravado he might use to embarrass me and his teachers.

I realized that on this day Lionel hadn't tested me at all. Instead he had gone out excitedly to get his data. *He wanted to go.* But not for the reasons he had used earlier in the quarter. He used to stretch us as far as he could in terms of trust. He was checking out *our* limits earlier. Now he was shifting to check out his own. As we chatted about his data the fact came out that all the cars had been locked. I wondered how Lionel got into the cars and he grinned. "Jus' let me know if you ever lock yourself out of *your* car."

In the next ten days I spent in that school I found that Lionel was a real leader. He had strength in many areas but had been labeled a delinquent by a host of people who spent inordinate amounts of time telling Lionel he could trust them — and almost at once contradicting their words with their actions. They spoke privately of Lionel as "deprived" and one whose "basic needs" were not being met. All in all they painted a pretty bleak picture of a fairly together person. I saw far more equilibrium in Lionel than I saw in many of the adults who judged him.

In other words, Lionel had a great metaphoric mind.

Many of the psychologists whom I had read and with whom I worked linked human motivation to needs. The more complex the theories, the more numerous the needs an individual would presumably attempt to fulfill. Most often these presumed needs were so culture-dependent that black kids like Lionel were automatically thought to be "deprived." Educators and psychologists would make such an assessment and then try to suggest how to fulfill these imagined needs. Their goal was usually to make "ghetto" dwellers acceptable by middle class cultural standards. Invariably their suggestions would reflect long lists of rational criteria that few of the street-smart folks valued.

149

In other words, values were in more conflict than needs. And, I strongly suspect, so were hemisphere preferences. By this I mean that left-hemisphere-dominant, rational types were effectively in control of right-hemisphere-dominant, metaphoric thinkers. Book-smart was locked in combat with street-smart. To try to understand this better I began pursuing value-motivation bases instead of the traditional "need" theories of motivation.

What I came to realize is that if I had been trained to see apples, I was an imbecile when it came to finding oranges. In other words the contexts varied. I was trained in one context, and the kids were experienced in another. Contexts are frameworks within which ideas and actions can be judged. If my context was framed in the idea of a "need" theory, then I had to be responsible for using a context that may have come from a different culture than the people with whom I was spending time. Many Anglo social scientists, for instance, whose value contexts are linked to acquisition of material possessions, are bewildered by the ascetic interior of many Native American homes in the Southwest. The social scientists' value of the need for power and security was often related to acquired "stuff." Obviously the more austere Native Americans (so the interpretation might go) did not have that need fulfilled.

Contexts differ but *basic* needs are the same for everyone. It was Maslow's *higher*-order needs that provided a series of criteria that were hard to pin down. What really were beauty, order, and goodness if the cultures differed? This is where I found myself clinging to the definitions of needs that were linked to my own upbringing. My context for these "needs" was that of the dominant white culture. And what *my* context valued as power, logic, goodness, and beauty did not match up to Lionel's.

The dominant white culture has a context of power, rationality, and logic and focuses on a familiar suite of value-prejudices. The "street-smart" context that Lionel was party to had quite different value-prejudices. And this street-smart context was widely subscribed to in the specialized culture of the urban minority. *It was typified by tolerance of the tentative, of ambiguity, and of a much wider presence of metaphor.*

Confusion emerged when I heard dominant-culture members and minority members who had left the neighborhoods say that the two groups manifest different "motivations." I saw no such difference but rather a difference in the contexts. Motivationally, I saw the minority black culture express a hope for those human qualities that the dominant culture cherished. They too wanted power, beauty, goodness and all the rest of Maslow's list.

Lionel and many like him were victims of conflict between contexts, not differences in motivation. When the contexts differ there is a tendency to confuse stimulation and motivation. It is far easier to focus on the extrinsic, the cultural ecology, when coming to conclusions about why people do what they do, rather than to take the time to really link behavior with their intrinsic motivation. This was illustrated by my tendency to judge Lionel's behavior in terms of *my* motivational context rather than his.

Again . . . the contexts. The white middle-class context has almost religiously accepted the rational logical modes of the left hemisphere. And remember the culture that defines logic defines ethic as well. The white middle-class cultural bloc has historically discriminated against right hemisphere and metaphoric functions. In the political and economic arenas as well, power-rooted discrimination has taken place. The power bloc has maintained the separation of contexts so well that minorities have been excluded from the "haves" context with ease. Unemployment and low per-capita income are the results of such context control. *These many factors affect the access to the context, but not the basic motivation of either group.* Minorities, locked out of the contexts of the dominant culture, have been falsely judged to be inferior in motivation. The same can be said of women and men, to the extent that they have been presumed to aspire to different goals and satisfactions.

It is my belief that *motivationally* all humans want valid things. They want the entire list of Maslow's needs to be accessible to them. Further, I believe all cultures wish to retain the right to determine their personal nuances of meaning for all the higher-order needs. When the cultural contexts which may be economic and political vary, then care must be taken not to conclude that disparities in behavior are caused by differences in motivation. Children, women, and men all want valid life. These are human as well as biological contexts.

What then are the qualities of *intrinsic* motivation? Maslow's "basic needs?" The higher needs? Any of a dozen answers can be given, and mine is not new. In fact there are overtones of Plato, Freud, Jung, and certainly Maslow in the "context" that provides me with the most functional metaphors for intrinsic motivation. I see them as the basic human tendencies related to INTELLECTUALITY, EMOTIONALITY, and SEXUALITY. I have used these words earlier in the book, but here I would like to elaborate upon them. Their general meanings will give way to more specific ones here. And I will define them as *motivational media*. They are qualities that I believe are neutral to culture but basic to humans. To my mind they are the most functional qualities through which motivation can truly be linked to behavior. It is through these qualities that humans express themselves as uniquely human. First to the definitions.

INTELLECTUALITY. Humans and cetacea (porpoises and their relatives) have the proportionally fattest bulbs on the ends of their nerve networks of all known creatures. It is folly to suggest that this does not create a unique capacity in these creatures. The brain works. It thinks, it invents, it verifies, and does a whole host of things beyond keeping the organism alive. Humans would think even if they tried not to. The mind plays incredible games with the universe, some of them rational, some metaphoric. Humans can engage in playfulness and joy or drudgery and (a word we commonly use) . . . work. Humans have little choice but to be motivated to think. They want to engage in intellectuality. It is a genetic mandate of the species.

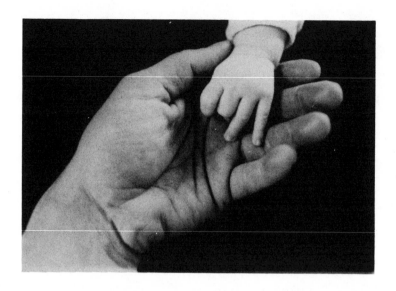

EMOTIONALITY. Humans are also motivated to feel. Emotionality, thought by some to be genetically mandated like intellectuality, appears also to be a characteristic medium of motivation. The urge to feel seems far more elusive and capricious than the urge to think. Elitists of rationality link objectivity and subjectivity to these two motivations. Objectivity is wedded to intellectuality and subjectivity to emotionality. This differentiation is simply an intellectual trick. Subjectivity is closely linked to rationality and objectivity to emotionality. Any serious attempt to separate these categorically is folly. Both intellectuality and emotionality are enriched by tacit as well as explicit experience. When feelings are relentlessly pursued by the rational-dominant medium of language, they often seem to wane and diminish in strength. But they are real. Feeling has been called by poets the life blood of human existence. Scientists have considered it to be static in the purity of thought. As a result, volumes have been created by intellectuals that both celebrate and denigrate its existence. To the psychologist emotionality is an incredible source of motivation in humans. Its role in the affairs of the person is no more or less important than the other two postures, intellectuality and sexuality.

155

SEXUALITY. My definition of sexuality is more holistic than the narrow concept of genitality. As I commented earlier, I feel it is accurate to define sexuality as the motivational characteristic that persists when the entire body is used as a medium of experience. This would include dancing, skiing, running, touching, sculpting, as well as sawing, hammering, looking and, oh yes, copulating. Sexuality is sensual. When the body is urged to participate with the universe, it creates access routes for emotionality and intellectuality as well. (Recall examples in Chapter 9 about how knowing is locked into the body and can be retrieved by resurrecting the sexuality of the body.) In a sense, intellectuality has invented extensions of the basic human sexuality to allow a more refined, a more detailed kind of exploration of the universe. These are sensory or motor amplifiers. Telescopes, microscopes, airplanes, spacecraft, and of course the hammers, saws, skis, and chisels alluded to above. We are motivated to physically experience the world in which we live.

Now if these definitions are accepted, the argument that emerged from our getting to know Lionel makes more sense. The street-smart human and the book-smart human may have different external contexts, but the internal contexts are the same. Intellectuality, Sexuality, and Emotionality belong to the species not to the culture. Getting to know the species is much more difficult than getting to know the culture. Care must be taken not to confuse natural and cultural contexts. Contexts are abstract and tend not to answer back. So it is easy to confuse them.

Now that I have defined the triad of qualities related to motivation, anyone who knows the classics will recall that Plato claimed human behavior flowed from three main sources: knowledge, emotion, and desire. Knowledge had its source in the head, emotion in the heart, and desire in the loins. So little has changed! But the qualities of the cultural contexts since Plato's pronouncement *have* changed. Generally the technologically facile world has moved to a posture that approves of Intellectuality, Emotionality, and Sexuality in that order, with intellectuality more appropriate in the culturally dominated Western technocracy by at least a factor of ten.

Nontechnical societies have maintained far more of an equilibrium. They have accepted the motivation to think and to know, but they have not afforded intellectuality the priority that it has in technical cultures. Likewise, nontechnical cultures have a far broader spectrum of approved expression in the medium of Sexuality.

Without exception, higher levels of equilibrium exist between the three motivational components in nontechnical societies than in our intellectually dominated technical culture. This point brings us to the focal issue in discussing this three-part motivational context. If these qualities are thought to be parts of a triangle, then emphasizing any point over the others creates disequilibrium, disharmony, debilitating competition. For example, if I stress my intellectual development at the expense of the emotionality and sexuality, the result will be disequilibrium in some form of psychic illness. I will become a rational (that is, intellectual) neurotic. I will seek rational, logical explanations and may defend myself forcefully against all disagreement.

Suppose I choose sexuality instead as my medium for disequilibrium. Then I will move, sense, touch and otherwise overindulge in experiencing my world while suppressing my intellectuality and probably much of my emotionality. My exploring body will provide access to ways of knowing that are shut off from my intellectuality and emotionality. But my neurotic compulsion to use my body to explore, to shut out my mind, and suppress my feelings makes me a good candidate to be a pathological killer as I isolate myself from all other motivational qualities.

Emotional extremism also fragments the psyche. It produces the compulsive "feeler" who shuts off intellect and sexuality and becomes a perfect candidate for the encounter groups popularized in the 1960s. These people are so busy "feeling" that they are useless to self and others.

Having illustrated these extremes, I would now like to change course slightly. What happens if Intellectuality, Emotionality, and Sexuality *are* in equilibrium? What kind of person emerges? Such a person is quite close to what Maslow and others called actualization. Actualization isn't a state, however; it is a process. To bring the motivational qualities of my tripartite self into equilibrium I must become comfortable about the relationship between my Intellectuality, Emotionality, and Sexuality. I am satisfied that they are not warring among themselves for the sole possession of my psychic being. My head does not suppress my heart to enable my head and my loins to go on a predatory expedition of bedrooms. In turn my heart does not exaggerate my loins' last experience so that my head will rationally try to compete and say, "it really wasn't that great!" Nor will my loins control the other two so that my head knows no responsibility and my heart no compassion.

The cultural schemes prioritize the linkages between these qualities in a series of stereotypes. The red-blooded American male is stereotyped into the Marlboro Man and is expected to be intellectual-sexual in motivational qualities. But to show emotion . . . never! John Wayne is *never* supposed to cry. Women have gained the emotional-sexual linkage by default. They are supposed to cry and "body-up" on command. The priest or pastor gets the remaining role linkage. He is supposed to be intellectual-emotional and avoid sexuality entirely.

That these stereotypes are dying signals the reality of the cultural transformation we are all sharing. The reality and eminence of the individual and the natural are creating a new context. One that thrives on equilibrium. One that allows for differences within equilibrium. One that has a conceptual disdain for dichotomies and separatism. Equilibrium between differing motivational contexts becomes the new goal. Dichotomies and other forms of separation tend to fragment. The cultural transformation is forcing us to focus more on motivation than on the specific nuances of what we use our motivation to do. This means that there is an emerging acceptance of John Denver, Guy Lombardo, Stevie Wonder, and Helen Reddy *at once*. No longer is it necessary for black cultural contexts to be separated from the dominant white culture with differing motivations presumed. The profound popularity of the Don Juan books and Black Elk marks the acceptance of Native American contexts. The motivations are the same, but even the differences in context are becoming points of Anglo celebration and growth. The dominant culture seems to be smiling the embarrassed smile of one who has made the discovery that domination is basically boring. A new vivid kind of equilibrium is emerging. Holism is nurtured by equilibrium.

160

Equilibrium means just that . . . things are equal. In natural systems dynamic and static equilibrium exists. In one, balance is maintained while everything changes. In the other, virtually nothing of concern changes. Actualization is more than bringing Intellectuality, Emotionality, and Sexuality into equilibrium. It *also* means coping with the inevitable changes that take place in the world. Imagine the triangle of Intellectuality, Emotionality, and Sexuality as a maple leaf. When it's out of equilibrium, it tumbles in the winds of change. When it is in equilibrium, it moves in all directions — but flatly, as though floating upon an invisible pond.

The discussions of Core Personality, the cerebral hemispheres, and the dichotomy between the rational and metaphoric minds have all merged into this concept of equilibrium. The metaphoric mind probably houses most of Sexuality. The rational mind probably favors Intellectuality. Emotionality probably exists in both hemispheres. On the left it "feels good" with rationality and order. On the right it is thrilled by doing and exploring. One side celebrates affirmation; the other celebrates invention. And again . . . equilibrium nurtures the qualities of growth and strength.

Charles Hampden-Turner once said to me that the act of dichotomization was the original sin. Certainly there is biblical support for this: Man-Woman, Good-Evil, God-Devil, Heaven-Hell. Yet dichotomization is fundamental to the strategies of knowing that nourish rationality. Throughout physics, biology, and mathematics, the tendencies to divide and understand have been of prime importance. Thus I have my own sensitivity to the categories or compartments I have used in these pages. Equilibrium as a construct seemed boring to the Western mind and it early sought disharmony, discord, and some form of conceptual extremism. No one guessed that in equilibrium might be found the messages now rising from Black Elk, Alan Watts, and Carlos Castaneda.

The triangle of Intellectuality, Emotionality, and Sexuality provides ways to look at emphasis in our life focus. They are identifiable media through which we explore and assimilate the experience gained in living. Each of us is better able than anyone else to discern when any one element is underemphasized — or exaggerated at the expense of others. In previous pages I have listed a collection of the various qualities we have explored in this book. Extrinsic-Intrinsic, motivational-stimulational, Authoritarian-Dependency-Intrinsic, and cultural-natural are all lumped together against the styles of action . . . growth-safety and creating-conforming.

Each of these qualities of being has been introduced not to fragment and separate us into niches or pigeonholes, but rather to provide us each with ways of looking at how our psyches function. Do I look to self or to others in times of stress? Do I choose safe, well-traveled paths when problems emerge or do I step comfortably into unfamiliar meadows of mind? Do I trust my metaphoric mind or am I compelled to seek reason in all I do? Do I spend my life waiting for it to happen to me or do I step out and guide its course?

Stated in the framework of these questions I hope that the categories I have presented do not seem like a bewildering collection of rational tricks in disguise. This book *is* after all about the *metaphoric* mind. But here lies the root of it all . . . *all* is metaphor. None of the laws of science, the truths of the ages, the meanings of existence are more than metaphors. Science chooses its metaphors in a particular medium just as poetry does. They *are* different. Or are they? The metaphors of science tend to limit meanings to concepts with widely agreed upon and specific meanings. In poetry, quite the opposite is true. The words chosen are those with the most holistic and generalizable of accepted meanings. Thus two sorts of freedoms simultaneously emerge. A category or term or metaphor can limit, or it can extend.

I suggest using these metaphors of process, of category, and of attitude just as you would use food. Ingest them, digest them, and be nourished by them. But like food, ideas only last so long. The ones that last the longest are the most holistic metaphors. Most readily discarded are the specific metaphors. If the metaphors I have chosen to describe these human qualities nourish you, partake of them until your tastes change . . . then move into other flavors, other worlds.

Human freedom includes freedom to *create* the metaphors by which we live, then to *choose* whether these metaphors limit or extend. All ideas can be tools or weapons. It is the choice that makes the difference.

On the beautiful trail I am, with it I wander.

—Navajo song

the fourth dimension
– another short editorial

Actualization is having the courage to be the gods within us. All the philosophies and psychologies of triumph in human experience share this sense of completeness, from which none of the qualities of humanness are excluded. Intellectuality, emotionality and sexuality . . . all are servant, all are master. In such synergic fulfillment the concepts of servant and master disappear. There is only oneness.

At moments of enlightenment the boundaries dissolve, the distinctions fade. Qualities of motivation such as Intellectuality, Emotionality, and Sexuality merge into a unity that defies separation. What does it matter what motivates as long as the inner winds of growth blow warm against the boundaries of our being? When the metaphoric mind is acknowledged, accepted, and celebrated, there is no longer a distinction between rational and metaphoric minds. There is only *mind.*

Many cultures have preserved within their cultural heritage an awareness of these concepts. But seldom have their thoughts translated well into our Western technocratic culture. There abound Native American philosophies with a world view far more intimately linking humans and the natural than ours allows. Sufis have brought images of triumph and absurdity to everyday life and wedded them powerfully. Consider this paraphrase:

> The mulla Nasrudin was busily searching about on his hands and knees in the dirt in front of his house.
> "What are you looking for, Mulla?" asked a friend.
> "My buttons . . . my buttons . . . I've lost my buttons," the mulla answered with vexation.
> "Where did you lose them, Mulla?"
> "Back there . . . back there in my house," said Nasrudin, angrily pointing into his house.
> "Well . . . why do you search here?" asked the puzzled friend.
> Nasrudin answered, "Because the light is so much better!"

This story is a perfect metaphor for the history of astronomy. For centuries, astronomers have searched the heavens looking for light. When they stopped, *then* they discovered such phenomena as neutron stars and black holes in space. The metaphors of light and darkness have for centuries been considered opposites, yet only a moment's reflection will reveal they are so mutually interdependent that they are one. As a culture we so often look for answers and write our rules merely on the basis of where there is more light.

167

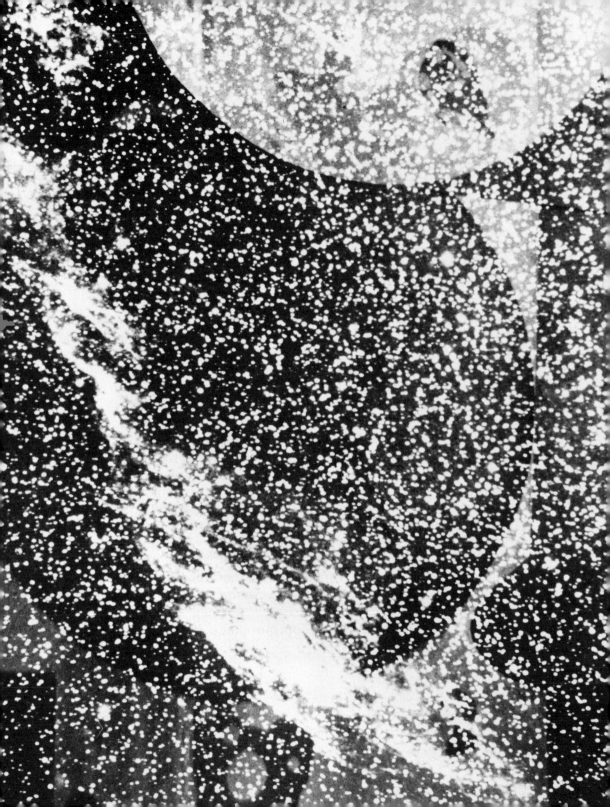

George Leonard tells the story of a woman who called a telephone talk show he was doing on television. He was promoting his book *The Transformation* and had talked on camera about higher levels of consciousness and cosmic awareness. He casually suggested that anyone who had suddenly "understood" something cosmic at some moment in their life call in and relate that experience over the air. For long minutes the phone board remained dead. George and the host tried to engage in a patter that would camouflage the silent board, but they kept urging people to call in. Finally, after an eternity of darkness, one line on the board lit up. The call was gleefully welcomed.

The caller was a woman from Kansas who had looked out into a growing summer night one evening while washing dishes and suddenly come to an implosive awareness that everything was one. She *knew* it! All the things in the world were the same and the differences were only superficial . . . all things were one. She paused, and then dried her hands and went to the parlor to tell her family. For them the concept was so foreign that they urged her to get some rest. In days to come, her insistence caused them to make her an appointment with the family physician. Frustrated, the physician referred her to a psychiatrist. In short order this woman found herself in a clinic undergoing psychiatric observation which eventually led to a voluntary commitment. After several months she left the institution and Kansas and moved to California. This moment on the telephone was the first time she had disclosed the story since leaving home.

Almost at once the entire phone board lit up. It was obvious that cosmic consciousness and transcending experiences are common in our culture . . . *but not commonly discussed.* Once this courageous woman broke the ice and awareness dawned that these kinds of "knowing" are not only fairly commonplace but normal, dozens of people were willing to call in.

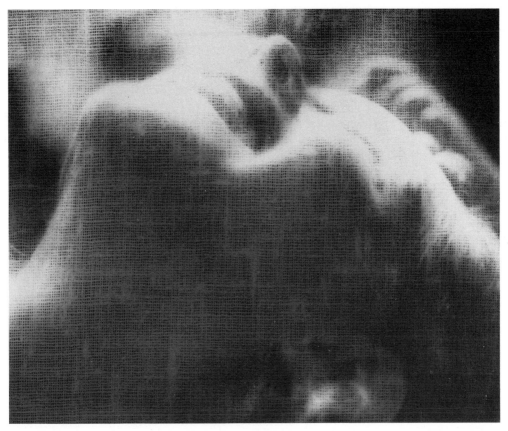

The peak experience Maslow talked about represents this kind of knowing. Women during childbirth often report a cosmic kind of knowing at the moment of birth. Lovemaking, discovery, and creative achievement are also common landscapes for peak experience. Whatever the context, the peak experience represents something to me that is quite distinct. It represents those moments when there is absolutely no distinction between the rational and metaphoric minds. Both are fully on and aware. They are both accepting and blending all of the perceptions and sensations they receive.

This kind of sensation is spiritual. And Spirituality is the fourth dimension of the emotional, intellectual, sexual triad. But the geometric spatial metaphor does not mean that the triangle becomes a square. Instead it is a tetrahedron. A four-pointed, 3-D figure made up of four triangles whose edges all touch. Spirituality is the peak of this little "mountain" image. Most often we spend our time trudging around the base. Once we begin to climb, the easiest route is often on one of the "ridges" formed by the edges — Emotionality, Intellectuality, and Sexuality. For example, most of us have experienced a spiritual or peak experience in Sexuality. Emotionality is also a ridge route to Spirituality, as is Intellectuality. These "ridges" are clearly separate in concept. But each *face* of the tetrahedron is comprised of at least *two* qualities. Our approach to the peak is more often on a ridge than along a face. Sexuality and Emotionality constitute one face, Sexuality and Intellectuality another and Intellectuality and Emotionality the third.

171

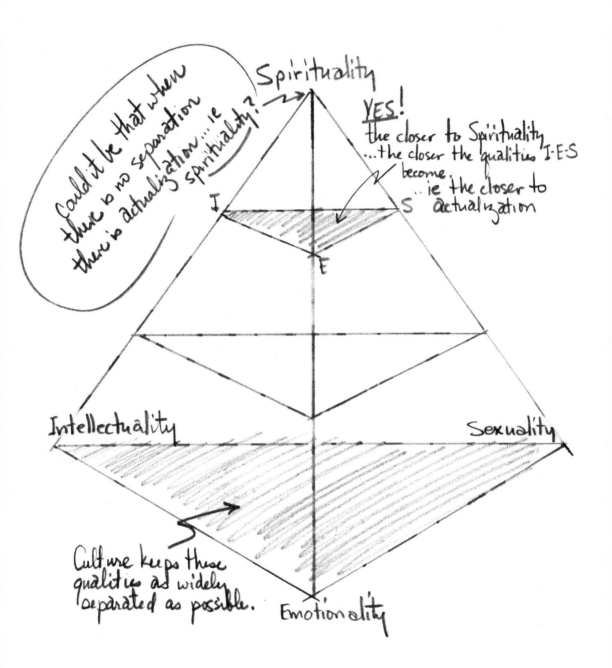

Could it be that when there is no separation ... there is actualization ... ie spirituality?

Spirituality

YES!
the closer to Spirituality
...the closer the qualities I·E·S become.
...ie the closer to actualization

I

S

E

Intellectuality

Sexuality

Emotionality

Culture keeps these qualities as widely separated as possible.

172

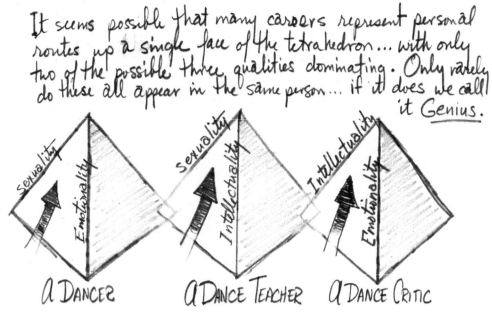

It seems possible that many careers represent personal routes up a single face of the tetrahedron... with only two of the possible three qualities dominating. Only rarely do these all appear in the same person... if it does we call it Genius.

a DANCER   a DANCE TEACHER   a DANCE CRITIC

The three faces can represent quite different approaches. For example, consider three people deeply immersed in ballet. A person seeking a peak experience in ballet on the sexual-emotional route might be a good dancer (Sexuality) who loved (Emotionality) ballet. One who chose the sexual-intellectual route would be a good dancer (Sexuality) who understood (Intellectuality) ballet. This second person might be a teacher of ballet. The third person would be intellectually and emotionally focused. This person might be one who loved ballet and understood it, but could not perform, a person who might become a ballet critic.

There is a tendency in contemporary society to separate the qualities of Sexuality, Emotionality, and Intellectuality in our everyday lives. Often Intellectuality is reserved for job or profession. Emotionality is reserved for family and a few select cultural institutions. Sexuality is generally expressed in competitive activities or lovemaking and is almost always carried out in secrecy or private, with the notable exception of organized sports or competitive athletics.

As a result, even the base of this tetrahedron has its compartmentalized quality. All of this is a visual metaphor for one image of motivational transformation. Our culture generally establishes the base of the tetrahedron. The triangles of Intellectuality, Emotionality, and

173

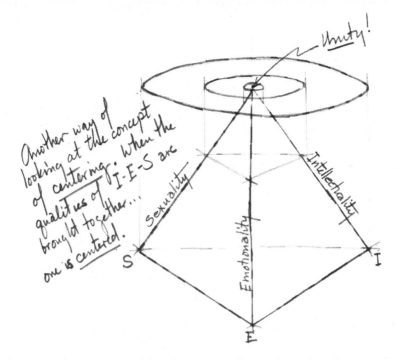

Another way of looking at the concept of centering. When the qualities of I-E-S are brought together... one is _centered_.

Unity!

Sexuality

Intellectuality

Emotionality

S

I

E

Sexuality are kept apart. Rather specific cultural rules apply to each. The higher individuals climb, taking either face or ridge routes, the closer together the motivational qualities are — each is treated equally and none gets automatic preference over others. At the peak they are one . . . a unity prevails.

Bringing these motivational qualities into equilibrium can be one of the true gifts we can give ourselves from a mental-health standpoint. Beyond the base of the image, there is the peak: the spiritual. But too often humans ignore or suppress peak experiences when they occur. For example, some psychologists would define each genital orgasm as a type of peak experience. Yet all who have experienced orgasm know that _each_ orgasm is not a "peak" experience.

People who engage in lovemaking with a human with whom they have deep emotional celebration know at once the difference between a peak experience in that setting and lovemaking that is purely sexual. Extending this, an intellectual conversation with one whom you celebrate emotionally and sexually is acutely spiritual.

Often we look where the light is better, rather than where the sources are. The potential for spiritual experience in any of the facets of our motivational being is always present. But far too seldom is it actualized. This may sound like a plea for a good dose of analytic-intellectual logic.

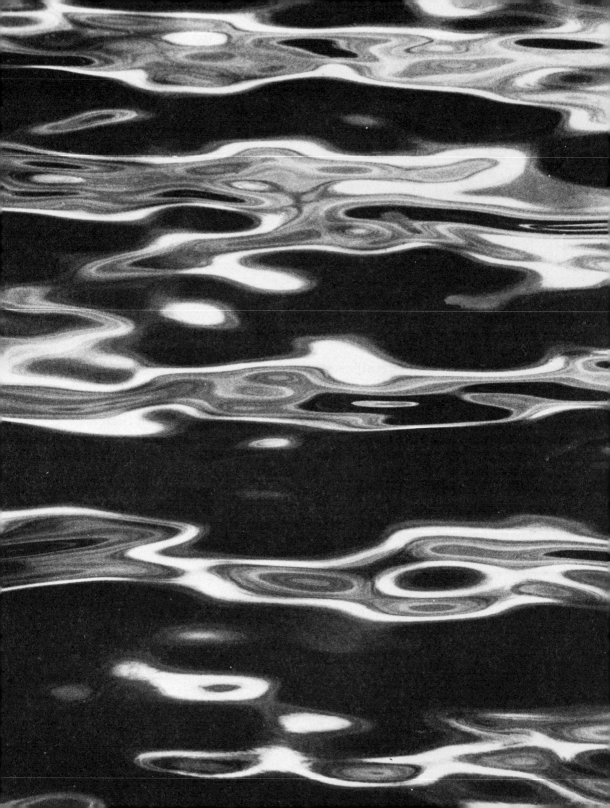

But it is not. My plea here is simple. Look at yourself long enough to know you are there . . . and then go as you choose. Look at motivation. Look at personality. Look at growth or safety tendencies in your own motivation. Sort out compulsions. For as surely as I go *toward* something, I am going *away* from something else.

Learning to relax within the rhythms of life is the greatest gift one can give oneself. To fully accept each facet, each process, that operates within us prevents our being owned by any. The rational mind gives us the gift of order, of logic, and of structure — metaphors to serve as temporary shelves for the clutter we perceive. These shelves are no more important than the clutter, but they *are* useful. And so long as the shelves do not begin to own our being, they are helpful.

Spirituality hovers lovingly above all our lives. Some are relearning the spirituality of nature, of art, of running, of dancing. Others choose to feel the joy of knowing patterns and order. There is no single medium, no single way. None of our routes is more worthy than any other. All the viable ways are characterized by the overriding quality of unity . . . synergy and wholeness. It is truly spiritual when the minds, rational and metaphoric, cease their warring . . . and embrace.

Knowing ignorance is strength
Ignoring knowledge is sickness
—TAO TE CHING

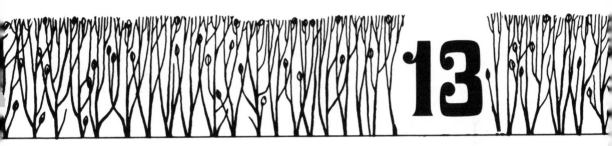

the disease of disequilibrium

In many of the earlier chapters I have alluded to equilibrium . . . the balance between the rational and metaphoric minds, the quiet synergy that exists when there is no attitudinal prejudice either toward or away from either of the natural functions of mind. Humans can reason, and it is as neurotic to deny this as it is to overindulge in it. I have emphasized rational neurosis because our cultural ecology nurtures an obsession with logic. The compulsion to reason, like any other, is unhealthy, though our minds are designed to reason as well as to dream.

178

In the past, therapies based on the differences between rationality and irrationality have abounded. In Western thought, Sigmund Freud was perhaps most eloquent and influential in sculpting the concepts that guided social and cultural definitions of what is "normal" and what is "deviant." Freud's meter stick was based on rationality and irrationality. Irrationality was compulsively unpredictable and antisocial behavior. Of course, "unpredictable" and "antisocial" are only deviations when compared to some norm. As it turned out, cases of psychosis were described by symptoms that were uncomfortable to Freud and were deviant in the eyes of the culture to which he subscribed.

Like any scientist, Freud could never be totally objective. As he invented the constructs of his theoretical framework, he was victim of his knowledge and of his culture. His knowledge was born of that beautiful post-Victorian era when the dawn of technological science emerged with the renewal of Darwin's and Lyell's theories of natural science. As Freud's early works were published, a young Albert Einstein failed his entrance exams to the engineering school in Zurich. The whole world of science was enjoying a rush of genius to its ranks. But at the same time, the specter of Victorian mores still shrouded the perceptions humans had of themselves and their role in the natural order of things.

Conflict between the church as a sculptor of ethics and science as a sculptor of mind had seldom been more pronounced. The explosion of technology gave science such energy that those who sought to be keepers of morality were forced to solidify their domain with fervor. Freud, genius that he was, balanced delicately between the growing scientific perceptions drawing him to classify, categorize, and theorize and the clutching forces of the Puritan-Victorian ethic that weightily tried to resist all new perceptions. On top of all this were the confused socio-economic energies of a society that knew change was inevitable but whose response was to thrust its feet into a concrete vision of history while pointing anxiously toward the future.

Perhaps it was the perfect time for a person like Freud. One who could take the completely shapeless mass that was psychology and with the tools of the new science create an image of humans reflecting the whole fabric of that cultural milieu. His images, powerful enough to last to this day, were influenced strongly by the cultural ecology of his time. Rationality as motivator reigned supreme. Emotionality was qualified: women and children could show it, but certainly not men. Sexuality was the cultural no-no. From the outset, Freud's perception of the motivational triad that I have emphasized was deflected away from equilibrium simply because of the prevailing post-Victorian ethic.

Strangely, the effect of these images of human motivation are still alive and well among us. In contemporary approaches in transactional analysis, the motivators of Intellectuality, Emotionality, and Sexuality find their counterparts in the Adult, Parent, and Child triad. Although transactionalists claim no priority for any one of these postures, seldom are they given equal weight in analysis. Adult — with its rational-intellectual component — always seems to get more favor than do the Parent-emotional or Child-sexual linkages. Thus transactional analysis may be a new technology for old Victorians.

What Freud really gave us is a psychological theory consistent with the philosophical theories inherited from the Greeks. Reason was King, Emotion was Queen, and Sex was Animal . . . Long live the King. In Freud's constructs, all of the qualities associated with the metaphoric mind were suspect. For him dreams were loaded with symbols of experience, experience that inhibited his and the Victorian's "spiritual" view of rationality. To him dreams were fraught with emotion, sexuality, and other irrational influences. Metaphoric language was considered an expression of latent disturbance. Capricious, spontaneous talking was either a "slip," (a revelation of a deeper, neurotic meaning) or an indicator of some mental deviance at war with the rational conscious processes.

Freud's greatest personal fears concerned Sexuality; accordingly, his premises of mental health and mental disease were replete with connotations of animalistic sexual drives. So anxiously did he link Sexuality to neurosis and psychosis that we are still digging out from under the psychological burden that his views heaped upon our consciences. This psychological burden, added to by the cultural and philosophical burden inherited from the sexual denial of the Victorians and the intellectual compulsion of the Greeks, created a setting in which few in our society could act upon any motivation other than rationality without feeling some sense of guilt.

Guilt is the main medium through which the metaphoric mind has been suppressed. Because rationality has had such a phenomenal historical public relations precedent, most people in our culture are conditioned to feel guilt about indulging in any expression of Emotionality or Sexuality. And since Emotionality and Sexuality are more holistic, more rich in variety, they are better suited to expression through the processes of the metaphoric mind. Freud's onus, passed on to us, was a psychological view of humans in which the metaphoric mind and its attendant motivators, Emotionality and Sexuality, were demeaned and vilified.

Contemporary psychologists are quick to point out the sexism in Freudian dogma. Freud described the human psyche from the male-dominant, female-passive posture so cherished in the scientific, moral, and philosophical ethic of his times. Some modern psychologists, not so satirically, are beginning to entertain "uterus envy" as a viable counterpart for the origins of neurosis in males to the more traditional "penis envy" Freud used to explain many neuroses of human females. Freud's sexism was a product of the prevailing form of prejudice . . . rationalism. Rationalism was the underlying criterion for mental health and it received full support from the anti-sexual focus of the Victorians.

Not until the 1950s did other psychiatrists provide viable alternative models to the basic Freudian theoretical structure of the rational and irrational dichotomy. It was nearly ten years after Freud's death that the metaphoric mind was invited into theoretical legitimacy, although Carl Jung had taken advantage of its richness for years before. Lawrence Kubie, a psychotherapist, was eloquent among those establishing its legitimacy. Kubie's work in therapy, hypnosis, and creativity led him to seek an alternative view to the extremes of rationality and irrationality as described by Freud. The Unconscious mind was the reservoir of irrationality. The Conscious mind was the residence of the rational.

Kubie realized that these extremes were not enough. Freud's Unconscious was a dark, seething cellar of agony, anguish, and evil. It hoarded neurosis and psychosis. It fed the fires that erupted into Conscious processes and disturbed rational thinking. It was in the Unconscious that Freud searched for the causes of neurosis and psychosis. Kubie agreed that Unconscious processes and Conscious processes were real, but his rejection of their either/or status caused him to describe a third quality existing between the two. This transition zone he called Preconscious. His descriptions of the playful Preconscious are elegant:

> The free play of preconscious processes accomplishes two goals concurrently: it supplies an endless stream of old data rearranged into new combinations of wholes and fragments on grounds of analogic elements; and it exercises a continuous selective influence not only on free associations, but also on the minutiae of living, thinking, walking, talking, dreaming, and indeed of every moment of life.*

The preconscious processes defined by Kubie painted a fine portrait of the metaphoric mind. Kubie further describes hypothetical profiles of people whose attitudes about mind function allow them varying degrees of access to these thought processes. Some prefer more rational mind function. Others reject access to rational process. The third group seek equilibrium and balance between these qualities.

*Kubie, Lawrence S. *Neurotic Distortion of the Creative Process.* The Noonday Press, New York, 1971, p. 39.

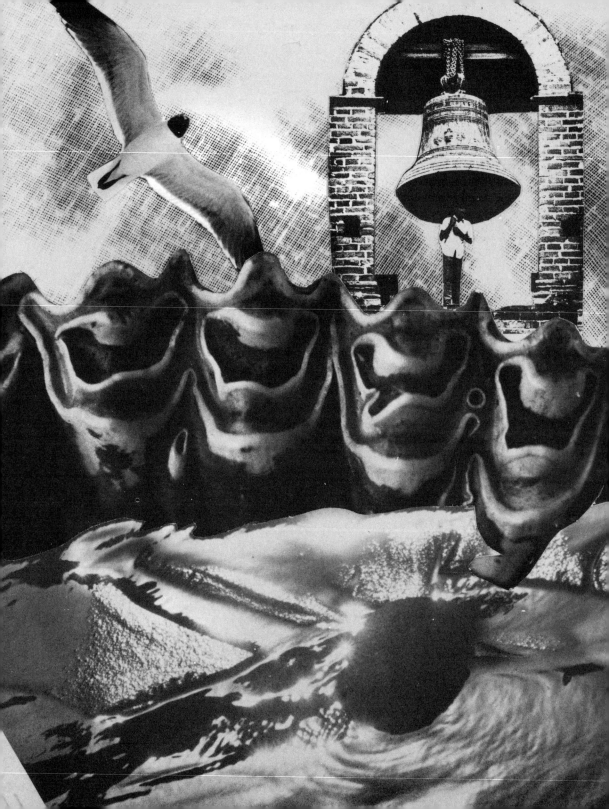

Freud thought that people with extreme rational dominance were mentally the healthiest. Those with irrational dominance were neurotic or psychotic. Further, he described those called "creative" as people with high degrees of Unconscious influence on their thought processes. Freud argued that uncontrollable mind function produced creativity. That is, the thought processes produced by this mind function were somewhat nonconforming and inexplicable. His bias led logically to the view that that which couldn't be explained was automatically irrational. Creative people reject conformity. Thus they exhibit a high degree of irrationality, according to Freud.

Kubie acknowledged Freud's views of the unconscious nonrational processes to a degree, but he did not feel they were the font of creativity. Kubie argued that the *preconscious* was that wellspring. He cited dreams, analogic thought, nonlinear processes, and holistic synthesizing as qualities of creativity. It is easy to link these to functions of the right cerebral hemisphere and the metaphoric mind in general. Not that dreams, fantasies, and analogies are to be judged wholly as *content*. They should also be seen as process. Content-focused people like Freud would feel that the modes of knowing common to dreams and fantasies were deviant. Because of the capricious combination of images, anyone who focused on content would discover deviance. But if one focused on process, the dream juxtaposition of a dead relation and a contemporary scene for the dreamer would not be considered deviant at all.

In my work it has become apparent to me that in such activities as dreaming and fantasizing, those who participate only feel guilty (that is, deviant) if they try to thrust the content of the experience into the contemporary rationality of any context within which they live. Once in a dream-reflection session with a mixed group of teenagers, pre-teens, and adults, a twelve-year-old related the following dream:

> The place I was had long vines hanging down and they were so tightly locked together that they were like a wall. At first when I saw it, it looked like a hedge. I knew somehow that I had to go through it all. I plunged in. It was easier than I thought. They separated like the bead curtains that lead to my bedroom. I walked deeper and deeper into them and finally I reached a clearing. It was bright and white. The light was beautiful . . . then I saw it. It was a single rose on a tall bush that reached my chest. I went to it. It was pure white and as I looked into it from the top I could see it was filled with blood . . .

At this point an anguished gasp interrupted the girl and a series of "OOOH YUK's" punctuated the setting. She smiled and said confidently that not only did the dream end there but she knew what it meant.

In accordance with the techniques of dream reflection I learned from Richard Jones, each person then played a role of "dream poet" rather than "dream censor." That is, each commented on the girl's dream without specific analysis. Interrogation was not allowed. Also their comments had to be stated as though it was their dream and not hers. The "poets" had to speak in the first person.

After a short time most had come up with a spectrum of symbols that ranged from death, murder, and suicide to Snow White and the seven dwarfs, King Arthur, and Jesus. She smiled through all this and then with great joy told us it was day residue — the very obvious entry of a day's activities and experiences into the dream process. We waited . . . and she said with shyness and triumph . . . "I had my first period . . . I'm a *woman!*"

187

We all cheered and congratulated her, whereupon she explained the vines were indeed the beaded curtain strands that led to her bedroom. But, she added, they led to the bathroom too. It was in the brilliant white bathroom, looking down into the stark white bowl of the toilet, that she detected the menstrual blood. We all giggled about our "poet" efforts but then felt good. If the "censor" had been consulted we might well have gathered a host of symbols to link the dream experience to some form of supposed "neurosis."

188

In the face of many such examples, I have come to ignore the universality of symbols in dreaming and fantasies so sought after by Jungians. Taking my lead from Richard Jones, I feel that the images of the nonrational mind are highly personal and cannot be easily generalized from one person to another. Thus dream researchers who take a what-your-dream-means approach are to be greeted with amusement but little seriousness.

As suggested by Freud and Kubie, unconscious or irrational thought processes *are* counterproductive to mental health. They provide a kind of mental shock pattern that draws the person out of conscious and preconscious contact. As psychiatrist David Viscott once mused . . . a neurotic is a person who builds castles in the air, and a psychotic is one who *lives* in them. A person who becomes compulsively diverted toward total preconscious or unconscious thought *is* out of equilibrium, just like a person who has a compulsive tendency toward purely rational thought. Being out of equilibrium is what constitutes mental illness. It is beyond the scope of this book to discuss the causes of disequilibirum, but most mental illness can be traced to three qualities:

1) Physical damage to the brain and central nervous system.
2) Chemical disequilibrium within the body
3) Attitude

Regardless of how these qualities combine to produce mental illness, there has always been an assumption that unconscious dominance nurtures creative behavior.

The most creative person is *not* dominated by unconscious processes, but rather one who has high access to *preconscious* processes. People who can get into their metaphoric minds and their rational minds with equal facility are the ones Kubie thought most creative. Kubie pointed out that unconscious dominance and floods of irrational thought are destructive to the creative person. Thus he denied the myth that you have to be a little crazy to be creative.

189

This view has enough romantic appeal for some creative people to play an aberrant and deviant to keep up their image! But this is as often a chosen ritual as a forced one. My work with highly creative people for the past ten years has convinced me that creative people are generally far more in equilibrium than either their rationally or irrationally dominated counterparts.

The image of mental health that I favor is one in which both capacities, the rational and the metaphoric, are legitimate. It is an image of equal access to the functions of both cerebral hemispheres and to the mind functions celebrated by both. The joy of closure and convergent mind function is only matched by the joy of new metaphoric nonvergent discovery. When both of these capacities are considered legitimate and celebrated fully, the synergic mind prevails. Synergy occurs when all things work together so that the sum of the energy in a system exceeds the total of the parts. There is a magic "catalyst" that makes things work better than they otherwise would.

True . . . this claim smacks strongly of mysticism and faith . . . but it is a quality of nature that tantalizes scientists at every turn as they seek knowledge of the physical world. Those who study the nature of the nuclei of atoms have known for decades that the forces holding the parts of atomic nuclei together are greater than can be accounted for by standard knowings. Confusion still reigns about energy sources for plant growth, the birth of stars, and the existence of auras and dozens of other transpersonal human phenomena. In other words, nearly everything significant that takes place in the natural world exceeds the sum of the descriptors we are clever enough to gather together to try to describe the process.

The most poignant statement of this was made by Lewis Thomas in his *The Lives of a Cell* , which won a National Book Award in 1975.

> We [humans] are not made up, as we had always supposed of successively enriched packets of our own parts. We are shared, rented, occupied. At the interior of the cells . . . are the mitochondria, and in a strict sense they are not ours. They turn out to be little separate creatures . . .

Just as Thomas creates a vivid basis for the overwhelmingly complex and interdependent nature of our physical bodies, he implies the same unbelievable complexity for the senses and the mind. He explores "vibes," pheromones (odors thought too subtle to detect), and nonverbal communication. Is it hard to imagine a conversation with a human who retained the ability to see auras, to sense pheromones, to detect minute changes in the magnetic field? Such people might seem totally distracted as they registered these "invisible" qualities that the over-whelming majority of humans would say did not exist. Their attention might wander. Their metaphors as they spoke might shift from colors and hues to smells and tastes, and they might shift about uneasily as they felt the energy nuances of an electromagnetic wind pass through their bodies. We might well believe they needed psychiatric care when in reality they were simply *fully* sensing through preconscious processes!

This access to holistic perception is what I refer to as metaphoric mind function. True our cultural system of preferences has created a reasonably distinct hierarchy of behaviors and performances for the healthy expression of rational or logical mind function. But no such counterpart exists for the healthy metaphoric mind. In fact, quite the opposite is true. Most often any expression of metaphoric mind function either in perception (sensing) or conception (thinking) is considered deviant. Freud considered this exhibition of deviance the interference of unconscious processes in the realm of conscious reason. Kubie challenged this. Though he did not recognize the structure or the diversity of the metaphoric mind which I cite in chapter 7, Kubie courageously defended its presence.

After twenty years of working with adults and children in the process of learning, I have no doubt that the metaphoric mind exists, though its presence is generally not welcomed in our culture. In hostile ecologies, those dominated by compulsive rationalists, the metaphoric mind is a deviant characteristic. It is treated as an illness or more often as a corruption of moral strength. Metaphoric mind function and those who display its operations are often spoken of by rational neurotics in the

191

same terms bigots apply to physically different humans. The culture describes the norm. That which deviates from the norm is asocial, acultural. Thus metaphoric mind function, which in fact *extends* the limits of the culture and its members, is often read out as the exact opposite. It is considered to be the destroyer of a culture. It comes down to the old argument of the Saturday matinee Western . . ." either yer with us or yer agin us."

Thankfully, woven into the very fibre of this complex tapestry called "modern times" is the very mechanism for survival that nature effortlessly provides in ecosystems. It is the germ of awareness. A silent but perceptible signal that drifts from the mitochondria to the galaxies. It is a message that fills each human with awarenesses that had been overwhelmed by the dominant static of the cultural norm-makers. Such a suggestion need not necessarily be viewed as mystical or religious. Another way of looking at it is suggested by Thomas as he acknowledges the structure of processes in modern (Western) science. He quotes Ziman, who says:

"A typical scientific paper has never pretended to be more than another little piece in a larger jigsaw — not significant in itself but as an element in a grander scheme."

Ziman goes on, "This technique of soliciting many modest contributions to the store of human knowledge has been the secret of Western science since the seventeenth century, for it achieves a corporate collective power that is far greater than any one individual can exert."

This is elegant testimony to the fragmentation-as-lifeblood quality of rational thought processes. The problem is that the level of simultaneous input about the state-of-the-art of knowing is getting so high that the compulsive fragmenters can no longer keep the awake and aware human from sensing the whole. The corporate-mindedness of contemporary technocratic culture *no longer owns the access to knowing*. The rational mind has played out its competence in hoarding the qualities of celebration. Its inventions of church, of law, of ethic, have all overexposed themselves. They were not statements of celebration but of confinement. Each has parsimoniously worked more diligently on *exclusion* than on *inclusion*.

192

Philosophy and psychology in Western thought have traditionally fallen victim to the games of the rational mind. The objective charade of simplistically knowledgeable philosophers and mathematicians in the seventeenth and eighteenth centuries is doomed by the realities of today's knowings. *There is no objective portrait of the mind.* This statement and this book exist to challenge the appropriateness of rational dominance over metaphor, not to deny the existence and appropriateness of rationality. My intent is not to build by destroying but to celebrate by unifying.

The metaphoric mind is a geyser whose pentup energy is about to exceed all the forces than can possibly work to contain it. Like the time when the child must emerge from the womb and be born, the metaphoric mind has emerged to the point where further containment is impossible.

The faithful servant rationality must now relinquish control in the household of mind. The creator is loose. Psychology, Science, Philosophy, and all of the authors of the formal, safety-motivated portraits of the human condition are destined to change. Educating, loving, exploring are all verb-forms that must lose their rigid, historical, constraining precedents. It is a new world . . . and there has been no war, no revolution, and no political action. There has been only the silent commitment of enough individuals to be human . . . *fully* human, that they have achieved and exhibited that quality of life. In that silence the things once feared as sickness — joy, excitement, anxiety, exploration, nonconformity, creativity — have all found sunlight. In that sunlight the human spirit now stands.

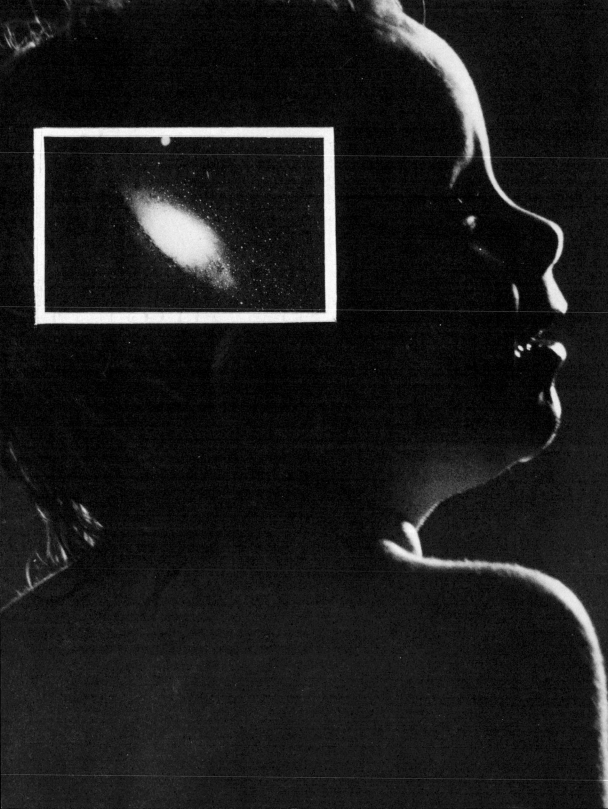

Inside the child, everything is moving. Harmoniously. The eyes remain wide open, passionately involved. The arms, the legs, continue their ballet. The hands endlessly explore.

—Frederick Leboyer

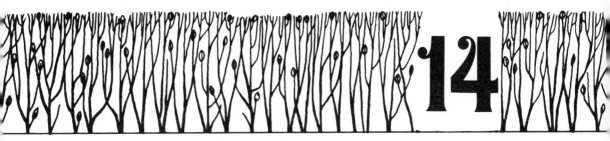

the new child

"Every star melts as surely as every snowflake . . . only to be born again in another time, another place." * In the sunlight of the inevitable changes that weave all things together, humans are returning to the systems of nature that gave them birth. Our foolish effort to separate humans from natural systems has run its course. The gift of the Renaissance has shown itself a poor gift. Enlightenment about the human condition is not based on conquering nature. How quickly that gift of energy became corrupted as humans "took" the energy of nature rather than celebrated it. The scenario is familiar . . . the human stands victor with sword raised, and the helpless victim lies bleeding at his feet (it was nearly always *his* feet in Western myths). The victim of the Enlightenment version of this drama was nature. The slave cast off the shackles of an old master only to forge them into the new shackles of the

* Line of narrative from film, *Where All Things Belong*, ESSENTIA, Tiburon, 1975.

tyrant of technology. The Church died and the logician won. Copernicus and Galileo cast the first stones of rationality into the quiet moats of dogma that surrounded the castles of god, but close behind them bent the new breed. Newton, Keppler, and Descartes danced in celebration on the graves of these martyred heretics, and rationality, the new mind game, curried favor among the ruling gentry. Contributions to the Church lost favor to contributions to the thinkers. The "knowers" became the new knights. Excaliber gave way to the slide rule.

Those waiting in the wings for a new kind of power to grab were gratified by the tidiness of logic. It was, after all, a kind of wedding of Aristotle and the lever. The new patrons of the intelligentsia were quick to fund the lever-makers. They invented an ethic of action. They were to pry the power away from the church and eventually give it to the computer.

Now the cycle has been completed. The technocratic mind has rationally created the social security number and scan-competent alphabets. Electrons no longer satisfied to shroud atomic nuclei zip about in servitude to those who believe the Hancock Tower in Chicago is *really* a challenge to the Matterhorn. For an embarrassingly short time, the window washer tried to become the new mountain-climbing hero, but no one believed it. One who stands on a window ledge to scrub technocratic filth off a steel and glass mountain is no hero. The role went back to the Marlboro Man. He, at least, rode on something that was alive.

197

Don't misunderstand me. The Renaissance wasn't all bad. But the legitimacy of verbs and action-oriented people was reinstated just when the artists, who create for grace, were locked in social combat with the rational technologists, who created for advantage. In the wake of that disequilibrium of purpose the scientists, whose self-avowed purpose was to seduce nature into revealing the secrets of order, became their own victims. So simple and so eloquent was the game of order-making that the humans who played it forgot that they — not nature — created the order. Michael Novak once wrote:

> Objectivity, in short, has the logical status of a myth: it builds up one sense of reality rather than others. It is a myth whose attainment and maintenance demands of its subjects a rigorous and continued asceticism . . . Science and technology ask of their practitioners a whole way of life. *

The first shibboleth, the crushing sweep toward pure truth and objectivity, became a commandment to the rationalists. Their prejudice continued past the Renaissance and the Enlightenment through the economic-political amplification of their cause called the Industrial Revolution into the Epoch of Technocratic Dominance called modern times. That sweep resulted in a time-lapse image of the armored knight transformed into a B-29 over Hiroshima and finally into a MIRV rocket in a concrete silo in the Dakotas. Without abandoning the rational game of human aggressively dominating human, we now spend the bulk of our rational energy on human dominating nature.

* Novak, Michael. *The Experience of Nothingness.* Harper and Row, New York, 1970, p. 37.

This illusion of the technological human's supremacy over nature is manifest in what I have earlier called original sin. Energy *taken*. Just as most physical education programs in contemporary schools are a training ground for rape (male aggressive, female passive, competition the ethic keeping score), modern rationality is dominantly focused on separating humans from nature. Already the greatest industry in the world is record-keeping. Humans spend as much as half our resources keeping records about other humans. Scholars are ordained on their ability to manipulate the results of record-keeping into new records. Counting is the new game for people in technocratic industry.

Recently a young technocrat in a Federal agency smirked with superiority as he recalled the way his decimal-placed bureau had "executed" the proposal of a grant seeker whose energy was to be commited to studying nature. This rational robot gleefully told how the proposal had been killed because it wasn't rational enough. It didn't lend itself to computer analysis. It was too "soft-minded." He went on to say that data should be gathered in such a way that the ultimate product of logic and rationality — the computer — could process them and gauge their validity. He was reminded that the proposal was to study the way the human mind creates. It was to explore the metaphoric function of the human brain. He might benefit from recalling that it was, after all, *the human brain that had invented the computer*. This suggestion was too much for him. There was no answer at all . . . only a blank, unknowing stare.

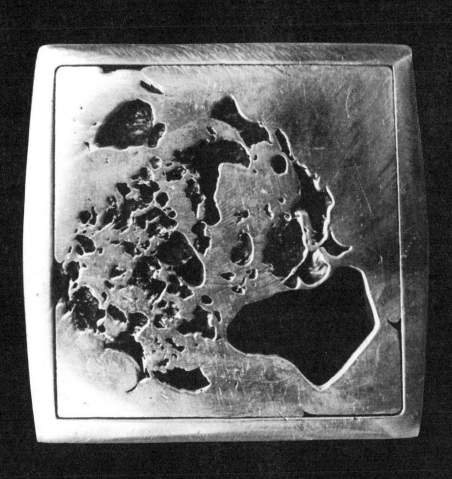

Lewis Thomas cites a growing bank of biological data that suggest that the concept of competition is itself a statement in chauvinism. Or a better word might be *speciesism*. Humans, following the lead of Darwin, one of the most influential of post-Renaissance rationalists, became convinced that in nature there was a state of competition.

Darwin's doctrine of the "fittest survival pattern" was quickly picked up by an aggressively competitive social system and applied to economics, politics, philosophy, and psychology. It is folly to argue whether Darwin meant what his interpreters say he meant, but it is rewarding to examine the gap between modern data and the metamedieval interpretation of "survival of the fittest."

Here Lewis Thomas's statements about the survival of the fittest in so-called "competitive" systems emerge. Thomas cites data that show that in what most humans describe as a competitive setting, *the less able organism begins to deteriorate in the presence of the more able rather than being conquered by the stronger one.*

This destroys one of the most sacred of technocratic mythologies. We do *not* need a shootout on the dusty streets of evolution. In effect, *the less apt just leaves town.* What agony to those who need winners and losers to dichotomize their lives! What suffering to those who are shocked into the knowing that nature does not tally scores. The decimal-placed mentality belongs to humans. It is the *human* values of finiteness that are threatened by infinity. Nature chooses not to care . . . or to care so much that *it doesn't matter.*

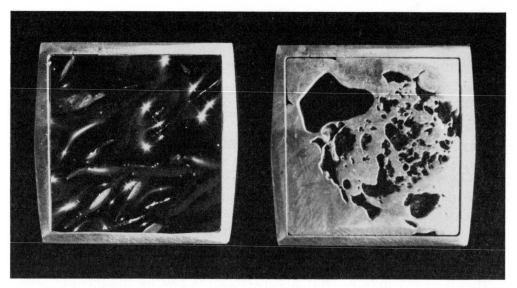

Salk's definition of wisdom is equilibrium. He hints at the depth of affiliation of what I term the metaphoric mind with the natural schemes. With natural wisdom. Cultural wisdom is aptly designated by the functions of the rational mind. Salk does not for a moment denigrate rationality and its competitive exploitative posture. But instead he celebrates the "naturalness" of equilibrium and how equilibrium creates a synergy of living.

From the Crusades to the last Superbowl and into the mythical world of "Rollerball," competition has meant killing off one's opposition. As long as it meant that, the survivors and the characteristics they possessed were considered superior. Or, "more fit." Jonas Salk has been the most distinguished spokesperson to challenge this illusion as he effectively describes a concept more aptly called the "survival of the wisest." Wisdom as Salk conceives it is equilibrium between the metabiological acts of aggression and passivity, between conquering and coexisting, between evaluation and acceptance. This final pair of characteristics relates to the form of aggression of rational mind (evaluation) compared to the more flexible role of intuitive metaphoric mind (acceptance).

Now to the New Child referred to in this chapter title. The new child is a metaphor for the synergic mind. The "wisest" as portrayed by Salk. In a brilliant talk, Carl Rogers recently said:

> . . . Man is wiser than his intellect . . . his whole organism has a wisdom and pur-posiveness which goes well beyond his conscious thought. . . . I think men and women, individually and collectively are inwardly and organismically rejecting the view of one single culture-approved reality. I believe they are moving inevitably toward the acceptance of millions of separate, challenging exciting informative *individual* perceptions of reality. I regard it as possible that this view — like the simultaneous and separate discovery of the principles of quantum mechanics by scientists in different countries — may begin to come into effective existence in many parts of the world at once. If so, we would be living in a totally new universe, different from any in history.

Robert Ornstein, the Beatles, Richard Jones, Ruth Benedict, John Vasconcellos, Margaret Mead, the Sierra Club, the Weyerhaeuser Corporation, and two or three people who live within shouting distance of you who read this are all speaking for the new evolution. For the new human destined to emerge when the whole mind is celebrated. We *are* standing in the sunlight. We *are* bathing in a new knowing. Humankind revels in the simultaneity of discovery. In recorded history there are uncounted numbers of cases where humans reached the same threshold of knowing at once. Each person reading this has discovered an insight into self, nature, or the humanmade world that was shared by one or more of the most remarkable minds in history. Each of us has suffered as well the caustic reminder by one less confident in discovery that our insight was first reported by Aristotle, Madame Curie, or Maslow . . . years before. The rational put-down was aimed at creating an historical harness for our metaphoric mind. A harness designed to keep us within the safe constraints of mindwork so that the record keepers could predict our behavior for decades to come with mythical accuracy.

The day that normative statistics were first described was the day of inquisition for the metaphoric mind. The bell-shaped curve of normative knowing pretends to be a system of inclusion, when in reality it is a system of exclusion. The norm-makers' charade of value-free description always measures that which *must* define a specific quality. That is, if I choose to measure your height, I assign a value to height. I must exclude your weight, probably your sex, and certainly I must exclude whether or not you like lilacs.

Culture's view of what constitutes normalcy determines what we describe as "knowing" and "reality." Our own vision of reality created the situation in which Don Juan Matus, the Yaqui shaman, effectively acted as a therapist for the rational-neurotic scholar Carlos Castaneda. Don Juan shared his vision of an alternative reality and led Castaneda to a posture of "higher" mental health. The Samoans were fortunate that a compassionate Margaret Mead chose to testify to the "therapy" they administered to her during her early years as an anthropologist. Because of her willingness to accept new knowings and new realities, she was able to rid herself of many of the biases of her own cultural

vision. She returned to New York and disclosed the Samoans' solution to problems Caucasians were wrestling with concerning puberty and the consummation of genital sexuality. That solution is remarkably similar to the sexual habits of contemporary American youth.

Simultaneity of discovery is part of nature. It is the energy that expands in human minds as they violate all the rational explanations of how dangerous it is to live astride the San Andreas Fault. "You will die!" scream the rational neurotics. "So will we all," say the San Franciscans. "The difference is that we *know* it."

Willi Unsoeld, as Director of the National Outward Bound Program, was once confronted by a pair of parents who demanded to know if he could guarantee that their child would not meet death in the hiking, climbing, swimming, and sailing the program prescribes. Willi, a sacred person, took a deep breath as his velvety blue eyes looked full in the face of the parents. "No," he said slowly, "I cannot guarantee the life of your child." He paused and then said with calm compassion, "However, I can guarantee the death of your child's soul . . . if you continue to protect him from such involvement."

We humans are going back to nature. We go with our full repertoire of cultural artifacts. Like movers on a harried day of changing abodes, we take with us what matters . . . we take with us what preserves our souls. The electric can opener is being left behind for the flower pots. The electric oven is stored in favor of the fireplace grill. The new house that was "just right" is passed up for the one that "lets me keep my cat."

In psychology, the compulsively rational attempt to preserve Sigmund Freud or Abraham Maslow is giving way to feeling better in one's presence with one's self. The vision of book-makers like myself is no longer the ultimate goal for all who read our words. We are just fellow humans whose arrogance and humility allow us to share our own perception of the journey into self. Others can look down the trail we have taken and then choose their own.

Synergy is stirring breezes that ruffle the pages of *Family Circle* and *The Philosophical Review*. The newsletter of the Kaiser Industries and this morning's announcement by the vice principal in Cherry Creek Junior High School east of Denver. In an hour your hand may water African violets or wield a scalpel to remove a tumor from the brain of a forty-year-old used-car salesman. It doesn't matter. We are all here together.

Therapy has been called education done late. If that is true, what we face now is a cultural, human ecology bent on changing the descriptors of both education and therapy. Education cannot be called therapy done at the right time. Instead we must acknowledge that the need for therapy demonstrates that something is wrong.

Suppose education is a process by which we share what is *right!* A process by which we communicate, with compassion, what we celebrate! Should this posture emerge, we would surely reestablish those vivid, vital ties with the natural. Alexander Marshack's notion of "cyclical time" and "storied time" would be reinstated. We would no longer fear to dream. We would celebrate our imagination and invent as comfortably as we verify. We would smile when reminded that something we said had been said years ago. We would smile in celebration that we were part of the natural human universe. What we do is what we do. There is joy and there is non-joy. Both cases reflect human involvement with the natural world.

No longer is human against nature or for nature . . . but finally human is with nature. The tidy mind that lines things up and puts them in order is no longer hostile toward the mind that creates. Soon humans can no longer differentiate between the two. There are no priorities to winning . . . to losing . . . only the priority of being.

Paul Tillich said, "Only when humans decide are they fully human." His words, a vivid and beautiful description of the elegance of being human, still echo in my mind. The message is complete if one envisions the whole mind in the process of decision — the mind of culture and the mind of nature . . . the mind of rationality and the mind of metaphor. But off of some distant surface that may be as near as my corpus callosum or as far as the most distant galaxy, echoes the rest of the message . . .

The Parent — nature and its mind of metaphor — is quietly, lovingly urging the child — culture and its mind of rationality — that the time has come to celebrate unity . . . to *live* the oneness destined by time's formless course. Humans are genetically destined to sense the vivid reality of all our qualities . . . intellectual, emotional, and sexual . . . and to blend them into a new vision of human spirituality. Spirituality will emerge as the end of competitiveness and the birth of an era of synergy. Species and organism, rationality and metaphor, adult and child will be celebrated at once.

Such is the androgenous vision that materializes in the womb of mind. Such is the vision of emerging spirituality. With no artifice of political unity . . . with no all-encompassing cultural laws . . . the vision appears destined to spring from the very strands of genetic fiber that weave our most fragile, most durable link with the cosmos. It is a vision enfolded in each of us . . . in the person . . . not the culture. Thus the transformation toward synergic culture will be the summary act of willing, personal rebirth. While today the competitive, nonsynergic cultures war among themselves, the synergic vision is unfolding in the personal spheres of loving . . . marriage . . . parenting. Competition, the negative version of unity, is dying. In culture as in nature it is seen to be useless. Synergy, the positive version of unity, is dawning in the human mind. It has always been with us . . . in the quiet mists of the metaphoric mind. In the pulse of the universe, the vision is being born anew.

. . . the seasons of synergy
are warming
in the sunlight of mind.

BOOKS THAT HELPED

Arnheim, Rudolf. *Visual Thinking*. University of California, Berkeley, 1969.

Assagioli, Roberto. *The Act of Will*. Viking, New York, 1973.

Bateson, Gregory. *Steps to an Ecology of Mind*. Ballantine, New York, 1972.

Becker, Ernest. *The Birth and Death of Meaning*. Free Press, New York, 1971.

Berger, Peter L. *Invitation to Sociology: A Humanistic Perspective*. Doubleday, Garden City, 1963.

Brown, Barbara. *New Mind, New Body*. Harper & Row, New York, 1974.

Bruner, Jerome. *On Knowing: Essays for the Left Hand*. Atheneum, New York, 1962.

Capra, Fritjof. *The Tao of Physics*. Shambhala, Berkeley, 1975.

Castaneda, Carlos. *A Separate Reality*. Simon & Schuster, New York, 1971.

de Bono, Edward. *The Mechanism of Mind*. Penguin, Middlesex, 1969.

Deci, Edward L. *Intrinsic Motivation*. Plenum, New York, 1975.

Dubos, Rene. *Beast or Angel*. Scribners, New York, 1974.

Eisley, Loren. *The Immense Journey*. Random House, New York, 1957.

Erikson, Erik. *Life History and the Historical Moment*. Norton, New York, 1975.

Fabun, Don. *Three Roads to Awareness*. Glencoe, Beverly Hills, 1970.

Faraday, Ann. *Dream Power*. Coward, McCann and Geogheyan, New York, 1972.

Ferguson, Marilyn. *The Brain Revolution*. Taplinger, New York, 1973.

Fromm, Erich. *The Anatomy of Human Destructiveness*. Holt, Rinehart, Winston, New York, 1973.

Gardner, Howard. *The Shattered Mind*. Knopf, New York, 1974.

Garfield, Patricia. *Creative Dreaming*. Simon and Schuster, New York, 1974.

Gordon, W.G.G. *Synectics*. Harper and Row, New York, 1961.

Hall, Edward. *The Silent Language*. Fawcett, Greenwich, 1959.

Hall, Edward. *Beyond Culture*. Doubleday, Garden City, 1976.

Hawkins, David. *The Language of Nature*. Freeman, San Francisco, 1964.

Hoffer, Eric. *The True Believer*. Harper & Row, New York, 1951.

Hoffman, Banesh. *Albert Einstein, Creator and Rebel*. New American Library, New York, 1972.

Illich, Ivan. *Tools for Conviviality*. Harper & Row, New York, 1973.

Jones, Richard M. *Fantasy and Feeling in Education*. Harper & Row, New York, 1968.

Jones, Richard M. *The New Psychology of Dreaming*. Grune and Stratton, New York, 1970.

Kluckhohn, Clyde and Dorthea Leighton. *The Navajo*. Doubleday, Garden City, 1962.

Koestler, Arthur. *The Act of Creation*. Macmillan, New York, 1964.

Kubie, Lawrence S. *Neurotic Distortion of the Creative Process*. Noonday, New York, 1958.

Leboyer, Frederick. *Birth Without Violence*. Knopf, New York, 1975.

Lee, Philip R., et al. *Symposium on Consciousness*. Viking, New York, 1976.
Leonard, George. *The Transformation*. Delacorte, New York, 1972.
Leonard, George. *The Ultimate Athlete*. Viking, New York, 1975.
LeShan, Lawrence. *The Medium, the Mystic, and the Physicist*. Viking, New York, 1974.
Levi-Strauss, Claude. *The Savage Mind*. University of Chicago, Chicago, 1973.
Marshack, Alexander. *The Roots of Civilization*. McGraw-Hill, New York, 1972.
Maslow, Abraham H. *The Psychology of Science*. Regnery, Chicago, 1969.
Maslow, Abraham H. *The Farther Reaches of Human Nature*. Viking, New York, 1971.
May, Rollo. *The Courage to Create*. Norton, New York, 1975.
McGlashan, Alan. *The Savage and Beautiful Country*. Houghton Mifflin, Boston, 1967.
McKim, Robert. *Experiences in Visual Thinking*. Brooks Cole, Monterey, 1972.
McLuhan, Marshall. *Understanding Media*. New American Library, New York, 1964.
McLuhan, Marshall. *Culture Is Our Business*. Ballantine, New York, 1970.
Niehardt, John G. *Black Elk Speaks*. Pocket Books, New York, 1972.
Nilsson, Lennart, et al. *A Child is Born*. Dell, New York, 1965.
Ornstein, Robert E. *The Psychology of Consciousness*. Viking, New York, 1972.
Ornstein, Robert E. *The Nature of Human Consciousness*. Freeman, San Francisco, 1973.
Ouspensky, P.D. *The Psychology of Man's Possible Evolution*. Vintage, New York, 1974.
Phillips, John L. Jr. *The Origins of Intellect: Piaget's Theory*. Freeman, San Francisco, 1969.
Piaget, Jean. *Play, Dreams and Imitation in Childhood*. Norton, New York, 1962.
Polanyi, Michael. *The Tacit Dimension*. Doubleday, Garden City, 1966.
Polanyi, Michael. *The Study of Man*. University of Chicago, Chicago, 1959.
Rose, Steven. *The Conscious Brain*. Knopf, New York, 1973.
Roszak, Theodore. *Unfinished Animal*. Harper & Row, New York, 1975.
Salk, Jonas. *Man Unfolding*. Harper & Row, New York, 1971.
Sartre, Jean-Paul. *The Psychology of Imagination*. Citadel, New York, 1963.
Schumacher, E.F. *Small is Beautiful*. Harper & Row, New York, 1975.
Tart, Charles, ed. *Altered States of Consciousness*. Doubleday, Garden City, 1972.
Tenhouten, Warren D. and Charles D. Kaplan. *Science and Its Mirror Image*. Harper & Row, New York, 1973.
Thomas, Lewis. *The Lives of a Cell*. Viking, New York, 1974.
Thompson, William Irwin. *At the Edge of History*. Harper & Row, New York, 1971.
Turbayne, Colin. *The Myth of Metaphor*. University of South Carolina, Columbia, 1971.
Viscott, David S. *The Making of a Psychiatrist*. Fawcett, Greenwich, 1972.
Watts, Alan. *Tao: The Watercourse Way*. Pantheon, New York, 1975.
Watzlawick, Paul et al. *Pragmatics of Human Communication*. Norton, New York, 1967.
Wilson, Colin. *New Pathways of Psychology*. Taplinger, New York, 1972.
Yankelovich, Daniel and William Barrett. *Ego and Instinct*. Random House, New York, 1970.
Zuni People. *The Zunis*. New American Library, New York, 1972.

ACKNOWLEDGEMENTS

One never knows the source of all gifts found in metaphoric celebration — so at the outset I am filled with the awareness that this list of acknowledgements will be incomplete.

Of the colleagues in conversation, written and spoken, these stand out: Jerome Bruner, David and Frances Hawkins, William J.J. Gordon, Richard Jones, Jonas Salk, Carl Rogers, George Leonard, David Galin, Robert Ornstein, Ken Peterson, O.J. Harvey, John Levy, James Halpin, David Kennedy. Jake Nice, Sidney and Toni Jourard, Sylvester King, Bill Bridges, Joe Drake, Dorothy Sherman, Frank Oppenheimer, Gary Pettigrew, Robert Burden, Jim Gladson, Gerry Kelly, Lois Knowles, Carol Tice, Bill Hammond, Charles Lyons, Carol Spence, Maxinne Mimms, Frances Clark, John Vasconcellos, Larry Rose, Bob Silber, Vin Rosenthal, Edward de Bono, Rudolph Arnheim, Robert McKim, Edward Kormondy, Bonnie McPherson, Richard Konicek.

Of particular writings, all the books listed in the section "books that have helped."

Of those with whom I have worked, Bob Lepper and Dick Barnhart stand out as the most prominent gadflys of the status quo. They were ably assisted by Gail Griffith Lyons, John Thompson, Bill Romey, Jim Lakis, Frank Watson, and Katherine Saltzman. In a special, kind, warm and accepting celebration stands Bob Wohlford, a most remarkable teacher-friend.

There were young people willing to display honestly their courage, fear, humor, and deep levels of humanness. These number in the thousands and web the country from Bedford Stuyvesant to East Los Angeles. From Fort Myers, Florida to Seattle. Among them, some brought gifts to my personal life — Kari Peters; Mark, Michael, and Glen Gilbert; Carol Sink; Kenny, Minda, and Tommy Wohlford; Rene Backart; Kari Mercurio. And now, in a live-in full-time celebration there is Stician Marin.

213

So vital to an effort of this sort are those very special people whose talents pushed loose-knit and rough-fibered thoughts into more gentle fabric. In addition to my editors at Addison-Wesley, I want to thank Lorna Cunkle, Pat Anderson, Kathy Parker, Sandi Peterson, and John Antonelli of the *Pacific Sun* in Mill Valley, California, who set these words into type with a kind of competence unmatched in my experience.

It is unusual to acknowledge the gift of an organization — but the Association for Humanistic Psychology has been an endless source of humans who subjected themselves to hundreds of hours of workshops, seminars, lectures, and discussion groups. These hours gave me as much inspiration to pretend to be a spokesperson for metaphoric thought as any. The AHP is more than an association — it is a vision of transformation. It celebrates diversity in humanness — and yet survives.

Of basic importance was the childhood my mother Eve and father Jean guaranteed me. They shared life in nomadic non-settled ways that took me from coast to coast, from mountaintop to tide pool and filled it all with themselves and love.

I find it difficult not to risk appearing flippant as I extend acknowledgement to the earth itself. Far more than hours with people, I have spent hours with the cosmos. I have climbed, walked, run, and swum. I have looked at, smiled into, and cried with the wind, the ice of timberline, and the stars. In these ways I have found the core of my experience with metaphor.

A special thanks too to John Denver. He understands metaphor and nature. He has sung the songs to me that so many times have blended my surges toward knowing with the simpler love I have for just being.

Though hesitant to end lists of this sort, I do so with the inclusion of those of love and strength who have surrounded me with their being as these words have emerged. There is Jan Rensel, whose presence is enough to transform any thing into more of what it is. Then there are Dick and Olina Gilbert, who rollick gently into one's spirit with warmth, competence, and complete acceptance. And there is Cheryl Charles, whose mind and soul have woven this book into an expression of her love for human celebration. It is her message as fully as mine.

Bob Samples
Tiburon, California